*Coleridge
on the Language
of Verse*

Princeton Essays in Literature
For a complete list of titles,
see pages 119-120

Coleridge
on the Language
of Verse

Emerson R. Marks

Princeton
University
Press

Copyright © 1981 by Princeton University Press

Published by Princeton University Press, Princeton, New Jersey
In the United Kingdom: Princeton University Press, Guildford, Surrey

All Rights Reserved

Library of Congress Cataloging in Publication Data will be found on
the last printed page of this book

Publication of this book has been aided by a grant from The Paul
Mellon Fund at Princeton University Press

This book has been composed in VIP Palatino

Clothbound editions of Princeton University Press books
are printed on acid-free paper, and binding materials are
chosen for strength and durability

Printed in the United States of America by Princeton University Press,
Princeton, New Jersey

Designed by Laury A. Egan

To Austin Warren

Contents

Preface ix

I Coleridge on Language 5

II The Language of Heaven 28

III The Universal Principle 42

IV Organic Mimesis and Poetic Art 60

V Tamers of the Chaos 96

Index 111

Preface

This little book is an outgrowth of a larger project that has occupied me for several years, an analytical history of the concept of poetic language entertained by men of letters from the Renaissance to the present day. That undertaking had a double initiation. First, its central importance was underscored by a growing conviction that the problem—for it *is* that—of the poet's medium is not simply one among a number of items constituting the general study of poetics but its very heart, if it is not in fact paradigmatic of literary theory itself. I am not the first to hold this view, which was expressed by W. K. Wimsatt and Cleanth Brooks over twenty years ago in their *Literary Criticism: A Short History*. Yet no full account of the successive efforts of poets, critics, and aesthetic philosophers to solve what many of them frankly regard as the enigma of poetic utterance has ever been written. My second motive was a sense that a history of the idea, an evaluative history such as I envisage, might provide a kind of intellectual clearing of the air, and so help future analysts to avoid certain confusions and contradictions that have bedeviled discussion of the problem from the very outset.

As my research progressed it became increasingly apparent that Samuel Taylor Coleridge was the pivotal figure in what progress toward certainty has been achieved on the baffling question of how (we may never know *why*) words take on added expressive power in metrical form. I became finally persuaded by the enduring cogency and penetration of his theory that it deserved separate treatment. The subject, after all, exercised his powerful intellect virtually throughout his career. No just assessment, nor even a proper understanding, of his conclusions is possible unless what is said in the celebrated chapters on poetic style and meter in the *Biographia Literaria* is read in the elucidating and enriching context of relevant passages from the public lectures, the notebooks, the correspondence, and the marginalia. And to do justice to the depth, complexity, and more-than-historical importance of these data clearly required an examination that would through its detail and extent take up disproportionate space in the relatively compendious account of the entire subject that I am preparing. Hence the present monograph.

There was something else. The brilliant discoveries of modern structuralist criticism gave a further impulse to my wish to devote special attention to Coleridge. In the face of the several crucial affinities between his poetics and what is probably the most rigorously systematic prosody yet produced in the West, my long-standing but incompletely examined sense of the lasting value of what Coleridge had done soon became a conviction which I hope the following pages will in some part justify. Structuralist confirmation of his linguistic and prosodic thought has a value beyond that of merely giving grounds for his admirers to exalt him as a pioneer thinker in this as in so much else. What we have here is a far more interesting if somewhat paradoxical situation not unknown in intellectual history. It is analogous to T. S. Eliot's notion of the poetic past being "altered by the present." For like other twentieth-century critical schools, such as the New Critics, who have claimed or been accorded Coleridgean lineage—but in a far more radical and dramatic fashion—the structuralists not only enhance the critical reputation of their Romantic predecessor (whom they give the impression

Preface

of never having read!) but even illuminate aspects of his prosody until now elusive to clear understanding.

At least as regards his concept of poetic diction, I am prepared to make explicit the claim some readers will infer from what I have already said: that despite all that his admirers have written about it Samuel Taylor Coleridge's poetics has not hitherto been fully appreciated. While making no pretense to having exhausted its explicative possibilities, the present essay is an attempt to supply some part of the deficiency.

Some of the reasons for this delayed valuation must be laid at Coleridge's own door. He is, notoriously, an inspired but disorderly writer. His distressing habit of suspending passages of the most admirably sustained argument to embark on irrelevant and often distracting intellectual ramblings has led many readers to sympathize with Eliot's characterization of the *Biographia* itself as "one of the wisest and silliest, the most exciting and exasperating books of criticism ever written." Besides, our modern predilection for cool and dispassionate expression in intellectual discussion is all too easily offended by the very different tone of the writer whom Edmond Scherer so aptly dubbed a *raisonneur enthousiaste*. Reading Coleridge is sometimes unpleasant and never easy. But for several years now students of literature have felt a growing interest in language as a human and social institution, and especially in its function as the medium of poetry. In the classrooms and corridors of our universities, in the pages of the scholarly journals, and from the lecterns of learned assemblies, the subject is being debated with unprecedented and almost fanatic intensity. And so the moment may be propitious for convincing at least some readers that the tax Coleridge lays on our patience is well worth the payment.

Like every other modern student of Coleridge I

Preface

owe a debt to Coleridgeans which I hope is duly acknowledged in the notes to my text. One special obligation, though, must be mentioned here. Walter Jackson Bate and James Engell, co-editors of the new *Biographia Literaria*, read the manuscript of this book in an earlier and shorter version which was the immediate result of Professor Bate's friendly prodding. For his warm encouragement I am especially grateful. I must also record my thanks to the National Endowment for the Humanities for their generous award of a Research Fellowship which freed me during 1977-1978 both greatly to advance my work on the larger project and to complete an initial draft of this book.

E.R.M.
Wellesley Hills
July 1979

*Coleridge
on the Language
of Verse*

I have strange power of speech.
The Ancient Mariner

I

Coleridge on Language

The prolific Coleridge scholarship of recent years has strangely slighted that aspect of the poet's literary theory which he himself thought centrally important and which, perhaps uniquely, owes little or nothing to any German "source": his conception of poetic diction. What little attention it has received is largely confined to how and wherein his opinions on the subject differ from Wordsworth's, with only perfunctory accounts, if any, of the theoretical grounds of the difference. Yet the first paragraph of *Biographia Literaria* lists "a settlement of the long-continued controversy concerning the true nature of poetic diction" among the book's chief aims. His epistolary references to the *Biographia* on the eve of its publication show that no other theme of that wide-ranging work meant so much to its author or gave him so deep a sense of significant achievement. A letter to William Sotheby in 1816 expresses his gratifying assurance that he has there settled the question "as far as Reasoning can settle it."[1]

After the lapse of over a hundred and sixty years it remains at least doubtful whether this claim has suffered superannuation. Or if it has, it is probably only to the extent that the problem has been further elab-

---

[1] *Collected Letters of Samuel Taylor Coleridge*, ed. Earl Leslie Griggs, 6 vols. (New York: Oxford University Press, 1956, 1971), IV, 620 (hereafter cited as *Letters*).

orated in the work of Roman Jakobson and the few other linguists who share Jakobson's poetic interests. Certainly the writings of no other critic before modern literary structuralism can show anything to match the sustained attention and depth of theoretical speculation that Coleridge brought to bear on what Thomas De Quincey was later to call the *quaestio vexata* of poetic diction. Quite apart from any wish to dissociate himself from the views expressed by Wordsworth in the 1800-1802 prefaces to *Lyrical Ballads*, Coleridge would have had to give some thought merely as poet to how and why words take on special value in poetry. But, for Coleridge, "to think at all," as he observed in *The Friend*, "is to theorize";[2] and if one's thinking about metrical language attains theoretical weight, it is likely sooner or later to probe the nature of language itself. It is therefore indispensable, as propaedeutic to a right understanding of his theory of poetic diction, to take account of Coleridge's unsleeping preoccupation with the phenomena of words and language.

For modern structuralists, whose speculations in any case generally conform to the grand paradigm of Ferdinand de Saussure's linguistic system, all literature is, quite simply, a product of language. "Toute connaissance du language aura, de ce fait," writes Tzetvan Todorov, "un intérêt pour le poéticien."[3] Coleridge would surely have agreed. His own lifelong interest in language went far beyond its use as an artistic medium, ranging from the most complex

[2] *The Collected Works of Samuel Taylor Coleridge*, ed. Kathleen Coburn (Princeton: Princeton University Press, 1969—), IV, *The Friend*, ed. Barbara E. Rooke, 2 vols. (1969) (hereafter cited as *The Friend*), I, 189.

[3] "For this reason, all knowledge of language will have interest for the poetic theorist." *Qu'est-ce que le Structuralisme?* 2: *Poétique* (Paris: Editions du Seuil, 1968), p. 26.

Coleridge on Language

issues of its status as an index of human consciousness to the minutest details of grammar, syntax, and vocabulary.[4] By 1814 he could speak in a letter to John Murray of his "long habits of meditation on Language, as the symbolic medium of the connection of Thought with Thought, & of thoughts, as affected and modified by Passion & Emotion...." No linguist today could lay greater stress on the centrality of speech generally to the nature of man and specifically to his aesthetic creativity. "Language," he tells Murray, "is the sacred Fire in the Temple of Humanity; and the Muses are it's [sic] especial & Vestal Priestesses."[5] The claim implied in the latter image is no doubt problematic. Yet it is worth noting that others, linguists and poets alike, have divined that the muses had a hand in the evolution of human utterance. The linguist Edward Sapir's conviction that language is "the most massive and inclusive art we know" has its more eloquent paraphrase in Paul Valéry's declaration that it can be regarded as "le chef-d'oeuvre des chefs-d'oeuvre littéraires."[6] In *Prometheus Unbound* Coleridge's younger contemporary gave the idea lyric expression.

Language is a perpetual Orphic song,
Which rules with Daedal harmony a throng
Of thoughts and forms, which else senseless and
    shapeless were.

---

[4] Some modern feminists will relish two entries in his notebook which lament the lack of an English common-gender pronoun to refer to a person irrespective of sex. *The Notebooks of Samuel Taylor Coleridge*, ed. Kathleen Coburn, 3 vols. to date (New York: Pantheon, 1957—), III, entries 3238, 3399 (hereafter cited as *Notebooks*).

[5] *Letters*, III, 522.

[6] Sapir, *Language* (New York: Harcourt, Brace and World, 1949), p. 220; Valéry, *Oeuvres*, 2 vols. (Paris: Gallimard, 1957), I, 1440-1441.

In the *Biographia* language is called "the armoury of the human mind," containing the trophies and weapons of its past and future conquests. Linguistic understanding, the discriminating use of words, was for Coleridge nothing less than the indispensable prior condition of intellectual progress and cultural health. "Words," he wrote in *The Friend*, "are moral acts," explaining some pages later that the ponderous metaphysics of that short-lived periodical was not intended, as some of its bemused readers seemed to suspect, to becloud their moral vision, but to expose the trickery of those who "abused the blessed machine of language." Favorite passages from Hobbes and the German philosopher Daniel Sennert, cited in the *Biographia*, Chapter XVI, and earlier employed as epigraphs for the third of the essays on Genial Criticism, trace conceptual error and confusion to careless verbalizing. Coleridge subscribed to Epictetus' doctrine (quoted by Sennert) that all education starts with word-study. In 1822 he conceived a plan to instruct a weekly class of select young men in the sort of knowledge which, as he put it, best yields power; and, he wrote Daniel Stuart, "the Root, and Trunk of the Tree" of this knowledge was "the precise import of words—the ready command, and quickness in appropriation of words—the principles and laws of Language, as the Organ of thinking. . . ."[7]

Exactly when the notion of a philosophical investigation of the phenomenon of language first occurred to him is hard to determine, but by 1800 at least he was urging William Godwin to write a book on the power of words. "Is Logic the *Essence* of Thinking?" he asked Godwin; "in other words—Is *thinking* im-

[7] *Biographia Literaria*, ed. J. Shawcross, 2 vols. (London: Oxford University Press, 1907), II, 22 (hereafter cited as *Biographia*); *The Friend*, I, 77, 108; *Biographia*, II, 22; *Letters*, V, 220.

possible without arbitrary signs? &—how far is the word 'arbitrary' a misnomer?" A few months later he addressed four long letters to Josiah Wedgwood attacking John Locke's philosophy. In the last of these (apparently never sent), he opposed to Locke's sensationalism the Cartesian belief that words can affect our emotions "without the regular intermediation of Images"—with implications for poetic theory too obvious for comment. The topic he suggested to Godwin later formed the core of his own never-published magnum opus on the power and use of words, described in a letter to Hyman Hurwitz as "an organon vere organon, or logic in it's living uses." This was planned as the introductory section of the grandiose philosophic enterprise appropriately entitled *Logosophia*, the work on which, Barbara Rooke reminds us, he hoped to ground his reputation, and to which, if we can take him at his word, he had by 1818 devoted "the best and most genial hours" of twenty years.[8]

From her study of Coleridge's two-volume manuscript *Logic*, Miss Snyder was led to conclude that he attached an almost supernatural importance to words and phrases. Certainly her synopsis of the manuscript and the excerpts which she printed with it signalize its central—almost obsessive—verbal orientation. His aim in the work is to instruct students in "the choice, connexion, and arrangement of words, for the purposes of distinct and conclusive reasoning." Part IV was projected as an "etymological history" of the term *Logos* itself as the name of the science that treats of "Words in relation to connected Thoughts." On the same page we read of "the high importance of Words" and of their incalculable moral and practical effects. In the brief compass of two consecutive pages of her synopsis of Volume I, Miss

[8] *Letters*, I, 625; II, 698; *The Friend*, I, lxxix; *Letters*, IV, 889.

Snyder must speak of "exactness in words," "the value of language," the "case for the linguistic arts," "the study of language," as well as Coleridge's "dwelling on the difference between λόγοι, or deliberate, carefully selected words, and ῥήματα, or the words of casual conversation."[9]

Modern commentary has just begun to recognize his linguistic speculations as, if not the centerpiece, at least an indispensable ingredient of Coleridge's intellectual system. In his latest book on language George Steiner includes Coleridge on a very short list of thinkers—with Plato, Vico, Saussure, and Roman Jakobson—who have added anything original and comprehensive to our knowledge of the subject. John Beer has recently pointed out that for Coleridge verbal communication was a constantly pondered miracle, a preoccupation to which Beer traces his abiding interest in the magnificent opening of the Gospel of Saint John: "In the beginning was the Word."[10] A detailed commentary on that Gospel was in fact to constitute the third of five (later six) treatises comprising the *Logosophia*.[11] But this interest ran deeper than Beer's remarks suggest. In Coleridge's metaphysics a hierarchical continuum joins ordinary speech with the divine Logos, so that the words which enable hu-

[9] *Coleridge on Logic and Learning*, ed. Alice D. Snyder (New Haven: Yale University Press, 1929), pp. 11, 74, 76, 78, 79. I correct Miss Snyder's misprint of ῥέματα for ῥήματα.

[10] Steiner, *After Babel: Aspects of Language and Translation* (New York: Oxford University Press, 1975), p. 79; Beer, "A Stream by Glimpses: Coleridge's Later Imagination," in *Coleridge's Variety*, ed. John Beer (New York: Macmillan, 1974), p. 235. Back in 1949 Herbert Read wrote that Coleridge's conception of language was even profounder than his interest in verbal styles. But he did not explore the point except to see in it an anticipation of existential thought. *The True Voice of Feeling* (New York: Pantheon, 1953), p. 179.

[11] *Letters*, IV, 687.

Coleridge on Language

man communication and intellection partake, though at a vast remove, of divine creativity. It is hardly excessive to conclude that the intellectual cosmos of his brilliant imagining and fragmentary execution was in virtually all of its branches essentially and pervasively linguistic. It is in some such all-inclusive context that his faith in "desynonymization" as a means of intellectual advance (to cite a familiar illustration) assumes its full cogency.

More than most poets, in fact as thinker and poet alike, Coleridge was fascinated by words. His unusual sensitivity endowed them, even apart from their meanings, with a palpable existence and a kind of personality that could charm or, in rare instances, repel him. He detested the vocable of his own given name, Samuel, which he anatomized with comic disgust in a letter to Robert Southey: "such a vile short plumpness, such a dull abortive smartness, in the first Syllable. . . . altogether it is perhaps the worst combination, of which vowels and consonants are susceptible." His prose, especially the correspondence and the notebooks, fairly bristles with coinages. Some of them, like the notorious *esemplastic*, are seriously intended to fill semantic gaps in English. A few of these, like *intensify* and *sensuous* (the latter not coined but rescued from desuetude by desynonymization from *sensual*), have entered the lexicon; most, like *securiorate*, *potenziate*, and *influencive*, seem not to have survived their inventor's usage. Others are merely struck off in jocular exuberance: *athanasiophagous* ("devouring Immortality by anticipation. . . . 'Tis a sweet Word!"); *vaccimulgence*, a mellifluous word for cow-milking ("I am pleased with the word."); *Theomammonists*, worshipers of God and Mammon. Yet even such verbal horseplay bespeaks a lexical bent of mind and is not unrelated to that rage for semantic precision that generated some of his more in-

Coleridge on Language

genious neologisms, like *escribence*, to designate written as against spoken eloquence.[12]

Coleridge loved to pun, a habit he laughed at even as he indulged it. In a playful letter of 1821 he gives his correspondent Dr. Gillman fair warning that "the *Pun*arhoea" is now on him, his mood giddy enough to be tickled by the aural identity of "leave it scarred" and "leave its card." But even punning was no mere joke. He once planned an essay on the subject and Miss Coburn calls our attention to his thought of writing an ode to punning! In Shakespeare's wordplay, an embarrassment to earlier Bardolators, Coleridge finds evidence that puns are natural expressions of anger and contempt. Those in Gaunt's dying speech from *Richard II* prompt him to the further observation that words are "a part of our life, of our very existence."[13]

For him, at any rate, they surely were. "How awful," he exclaims, thinking of Milton's description of poetry as simple, sensuous, and passionate, "is the power of words! fearful often in their consequences when merely felt, not understood; but most awful when both felt and understood!" This remark occurs in the lectures on Shakespeare, whose plays of course provided Coleridge with the most telling instances of verbal power in its most intense form, poetry. In a phrase from *The Tempest*, "Me, and thy crying self,"

---

[12] *Letters*, II, 1126; *Biographia*, I, 87, 109; *Notebooks*, II, entry 3112; *Biographia*, I, 189; *Letters*, V, 29; I, 557, 251; II, 1042; V, 514. The *OED* lists *influencive* as "apparently" due to Coleridge and cites only two other instances, one of them by his daughter Sara, none after 1857. Coleridge's apologia for his neologism was publicized in the *Biographia*: "Unusual and new coined words are doubtless an evil; but vagueness, confusion, and imperfect conveyance of our thoughts are a far greater" (I, 189).

[13] *Letters*, V, 185; *Notebooks*, II, editor's note to entry 3542; Samuel Taylor Coleridge, *Shakespearean Criticism*, ed. Thomas Middleton Raysor, 2 vols. (New York: Dutton, 1960), II, 104-105, 144 (hereafter cited as *Shakespearean Criticism*).

he observes how Shakespeare by the single epithet *crying* compels the audience to a vivid realization of the scene Prospero is relating to his daughter—an observation later borrowed without specific acknowledgment by William Hazlitt.[14]

Anything but pedantic, Coleridge's interest in language was broadly inclusive, giving equal emphasis to the oral and the written, the archaic and the current, the casual and the erudite. He was continually alert to point out verbal niceties to his friends. In a poem by Humphry Davy he objects to the phrase "sameness & identity" because the words are too etymologically similar to be juxtaposed, the etymology of a word being, as he thought, a part of its import and thus a factor in good usage. A note taken during his Mediterranean sojourn records the amusing despair over the difficulty of the English language vented by an Italian fellow-voyager, for whom *ship*, *sheep*, *chip*, and *cheap* were identical in sound. His interest in the history and primitive forms of languages was equally lively and discerning. In 1800 a reading of the Abbé Molina's *Geographical, Natural, and Civil History of Chile* occasioned his perception that the highly inflected structure of primitive languages, their "multitude & complexity of tenses," is "a mark of barbarism not a mark of ingenuity, as the Grecomanists babble," a judgment apparently lost to scholarly sight until its authoritative reassertion by Otto Jespersen.[15]

---

[14] *Shakespearean Criticism*, I, 148-149; II, 135.

[15] *Letters*, I, 630; *Notebooks*, II, entry 2730; III, entry 3789. In 1921 Jespersen refuted the notion of linguistic decay fathered by worshipers of Greek and Latin, for whom no language seemed respectable "that had not four or five distinct cases and three genders, or that had less than five tenses and as many moods in its verbs." *Language: Its Nature, Development, and Origin* (New York: Norton, 1944), p. 321. His own opinion, like Coleridge's, is the opposite of this view. See *ibid.*, pp. 322-325.

Coleridge was fond of pondering the peculiar "geniuses" of the modern languages he knew, and of classical Greek and Latin, especially as to their fitness for poetic or philosophic expression. He felt the contrasting qualities of the several major European tongues and tried to distinguish their peculiar virtues: German best for intellectual analysis; Italian the "sweetest"; Spanish the "most majestic"; English best for emotive utterance; French for conversation. Some languages he thought better adapted to certain poetic genres than others, although English remained unequaled for any poetry uniting deep thought and complex passion. German is best for translating the classics, though hexameters go better in English.[16]

These speculations in what may be termed comparative stylistics were recorded in his commonplace books during the first decade of the new century. The subject, however, absorbed him sporadically for the rest of his life. A single passage in a letter to Dr. Gillman's son James, Jr., written in October 1826, dispels any suspicion that these linguistic characterizations were merely gratuitous or impressionistic.

. . . the Latin Language in proportion to the quantum of it's difference from the English, as produced by the original structure of the words, has one disadvantage—or what is occasionally such—It is this: that in most instances you must have heard the whole sentence before you can ascertain the sense of any part—the last word or words being necessary to determine the meaning of all the foregoing. Among the modern Languages the German is nearest to the

---

[16] *Notebooks*, II, entry 2431; III, entry 3557; *Letters*, I, 450. Even Coleridge's pervading and unfortunate Francophobia had its linguistic aspect. In a letter to Thomas Wedgwood he confesses his comparative weakness in French; and "as to Pronunciation, all my Organs of Speech, from the bottom of the Larynx to the Edge of my Lips, are utterly and naturally Anti Gallican." *Letters*, II, 878.

Coleridge on Language

Latin in this respect: and hence neither the German nor the Latin suit well for Comedy or works of light wit and colloquial rapidity and interchange of thought.[17]

Whatever refinements of his method or revisions of his conclusions modern analytical techniques may entail, Coleridge has here clearly glimpsed the relation between the syntactical structure of a language and its expressive potential.

Although in 1799 he was boasting to Thomas Poole that he could now read German like English ("that is, without any *mental* translation as I read"), a later notebook entry denies that anyone can have more than one native tongue. When a nation adopts another language than its own, he noted, it undergoes an alteration in moral feeling, because language is "the medium of all Thoughts to *ourselves*, of all Feelings to others, & partly to ourselves. . . ."[18] There is a striking similarity between this observation and the views of the only other major English poet whose poetics rivals Coleridge's in its continuous engrossment with the poet's language. "A thought expressed in a different language," T. S. Eliot wrote in "The Social Function of Poetry,"

may be practically the same thought, but a feeling or emotion expressed in a different language is not the same feeling or emotion. One of the reasons for learning at least one foreign language well is that we acquire a kind of supplementary personality; one of the reasons for not acquiring a new language instead *of our own is that most of us do not want to become a different person.*[19]

[17] *Letters*, VI, 639.
[18] *Ibid.*, I, 453; *Notebooks*, III, entry 4237.
[19] *On Poetry and Poets* (New York: Farrar, Straus, and Cudahy, 1957), p. 8.

The common element in these two quotations profoundly challenges the facile parallels traditionally drawn between the medium of poetry and those of music, sculpture, or painting. Its implications go even beyond the occasionally voiced reservation that words, unlike pigments, clay, or musical tones, are charged with conceptual and referential value. For as Eliot and Coleridge envisage it, language is symbolic of human consciousness itself in its intellectual, moral, and psychological totality.[20] It may be worth noting, in passing, that this conception of language was far harder to entertain in the still predominantly rationalist intellectual climate of Coleridge's day than it had become for Eliot in 1945.

Moreover, for Coleridge—it is not clear that Eliot would go so far—language is symbolic in a sense not inconsistent with the definition of *symbol* which he gives in *The Statesman's Manual*, where it is described as "an actual and essential part of that, the whole of which it represents." Miss Snyder prints a passage deleted from an autograph manuscript of his treatise on method which it is suggestive to consider along with this inclusive description: "For the Word is the first Birth of the Idea, and it's flexible organ."[21] Since in Coleridge's Platonic terminology ideas have ontological status, language would therefore be in part constitutive of reality; but it would be difficult to show that so thorough-going an idealism represented

[20] Cf. Coleridge's objection to teaching children the grammar of a dead language before its vocabulary, since the habit of using meaningless words may lead to using words with false meanings, resulting in lies, duplicity, and political and religious fanaticism: ". . . Intellectual Accuracy is the faithful Friend, and next door Neighbor of Moral Veracity, so that both are comprized in the one term, Truth." *Notebooks*, III, entry 4210.
[21] *The Collected Works of Samuel Taylor Coleridge*, VI, *Lay Sermons*, ed. R. J. White (1972), p. 79; *S. T. Coleridge's Treatise on Method*, ed. Alice D. Snyder (London: Constable, 1934), p. 81.

his considered view or that he consistently held to it. The consequences of these linguistic ideas for Coleridge's poetics are by no means negligible. They do much to explain his hearty endorsement, in Chapter XVI of the *Biographia*, of Dante's belief that to maintain the purity of his country's speech is the poet's first duty, which, significantly enough, is precisely the "social function" to which the title of Eliot's aforementioned essay alludes. To assign the poet such a function may seem to trivialize his social role to that of a charming ally of the lexicographer or the grammarian. Given Coleridge's convictions as to the nature of verbal expression, however, the task of preserving the idiom actually exalts poetry to little less than our chief defense against dehumanization. It reasserts in more sophisticated terms the favorite maxim of Renaissance literary critics that poets are the first civilizers, and it elucidates Coleridge's own striking characterization of poets as "Gods of Love who tame the Chaos."[22]

The letter to Godwin of September 1800, mentioned earlier, contains perhaps the first reference to a cardinal principle of Coleridge's linguistic thinking: "I would endeavour to destroy the old antithesis of *Words & Things*, elevating, as it were, Words into

---

[22] *Notebooks*, II, entry 2355. Cf. Eliot: "I cannot read Norwegian poetry, but if I were told that no more poetry was being written in the Norwegian language, I should feel an alarm which would be more than generous sympathy. I should regard it as a spot of malady which was likely to spread over the whole Continent; the beginning of a decline which would mean that people everywhere would cease to be able to express, and consequently be able to feel, the emotions of civilized beings." *On Poetry and Poets*, p. 15. Eliot's atrophy of human sensibility resulting from the death of poetry seems not unrelated to Wordsworth's aim in *Lyrical Ballads* as Coleridge describes it: the mental awakening of a generation who "have eyes, yet see not, ears that hear not, and hearts that neither feel nor understand." *Biographia*, II, 6.

Things, & living Things too." That this aim stopped short of outright verbal reification can be inferred from many of his other references to language. The qualification is made most explicit in another letter, written over twenty years later, to William Mudford, in which, objecting to the exclusive appropriation of the word *Catholic* by the Roman Church, he concedes that they are "*Spirits* and *living Agents* that are seldom misused without avenging themselves. . . ."[23]

The significance of Coleridge's notion of the mode and operancy of human speech goes far beyond a mere rejection of the reductive instrumentalism of rationalist linguistic theory, whereby words merely "point to" or "stand for" mental images of existent realities. In the middle of the previous century Edmund Burke had already dissented from the "common notion" that words "affect the mind by raising in it ideas of those things for which custom has appointed them to stand."[24] The vital agency which Coleridge assigns to words actually endows them with quasi-autonomous value. There is an interesting notebook entry of 1810 on his intended essay in defense of punning (here given the whimsical title "Apology for Paronomasy, alias Punning"). He finds in the device evidence that words are not mere symbols of thoughts and objects but things in themselves, as he was constantly maintaining,

—*and that any harmony in the things symbolized will perforce be presented to us more easily as well as with additional beauty by a correspondent harmony of the Symbols with each other.*

---

[23] *Letters*, I, 626; V, 228.
[24] *A Philosophical Inquiry into the Origin of Our Ideas of the Sublime and the Beautiful* (London, 1812), p. 313 (first published in 1757).

He then jots down Latin and German versions of an apothegm attributed to Epictetus: "Heri vidi fragilem frangi, hodie mortalem mori; Gestern sah ich was gebrechliches brechen, heute was sterbichles sterben" (Yesterday I saw the fragile break, today the mortal die). In the assonances, exploiting as they do a correspondence of phonic and semantic elements which is lost in the English version, he sees a special beauty of what he calls the homogeneous languages. He had possibly been impelled to this somewhat hasty judgment by the aural charm of the conceited style of sixteenth-century Italian lyrics, especially the madrigals of Giovambattista Strozzi, several of which are quoted at length in the *Biographia*, Chapter XVI.[25]

Recalling that Coleridge's ultimate concern was with language as it functions in poetry, his constant preoccupation with the nature and behavior of language in general seems like an impulse of instinctive wisdom in the light of modern structural poetics. In an influential essay of 1960 entitled "Linguistics and Poetics," Roman Jakobson argued that the poetic function is not confined to poetry or even to literature. He instances a girl who spoke always of "horrible Harry," never of *dreadful, frightful*, or *disgusting* Harry. "Without realizing it she clung to the poetic device of paronomasia."[26] Coleridge's note ends with Julius Caesar's terse communiqué, "Veni, vidi, vici," as though suddenly recalled as a happily familiar case of that accession of additional beauty lent to expres-

---

[25] *Notebooks*, III, entry 3762. *Symbol* in this passage obviously bears only its usual meaning of *sign*, not the richer import of Coleridge's famous definition in *The Statesman's Manual*. This entry contains an especially lush example of Strozzi's word-play: *che l'Onda chiara/E l'ombra non men cara.*

[26] *Essays on the Language of Literature*, ed. Seymour Chatman and Samuel R. Levin (Boston: Houghton-Mifflin, 1967), p. 302.

sion by "a correspondent harmony of the Symbols with each other." And, in what is no mere coincidence of citation, Jakobson writes:

The symmetry of three disyllabic words with an identical initial consonant and identical final vowel added splendor to the laconic victory message of Caesar: "Veni, vidi, vici."[27]

The boldness and originality of Coleridge's remarks on language make it misleadingly easy to overstate the case for his anticipation of twentieth-century linguistic discoveries. We need to keep in mind that even his most advanced insights and inferences are methodologically divided from modern investigation by the rich and complex developments of nineteenth-century Indo-European linguistics and the even more rigorous analytical procedures initiated by Ferdinand de Saussure's famous *Cours de linguistique générale.* Nevertheless, the adumbrations of modern linguistic doctrine scattered throughout Coleridge's prose work do, I think, justify Robert Scholes' assertion that Coleridge is "if not the father then a genial and beneficent uncle" of modern structuralist poetics.[28]

At the very least, returning to Coleridge after perusing the structuralists is to be reminded, often startlingly, of certain fundamentals of their system. Consider for example the following from the letter to the younger Gillman already cited:

[27] *Ibid.*, p. 304.
[28] *Structuralism in Literature: An Introduction* (New Haven: Yale University Press, 1974), p. 179. Long before the current vogue of linguistically oriented poetics, René Wellek saw in the Wordsworth-Coleridge discussion of poetic diction adumbrations of concepts then being promulgated by the Slavic functional linguists centered in Prague. See his "Wordsworth's and Coleridge's Theories of Poetic Diction" in *Charisteria Guilelmo Mathesio Quinquagenario, a Discipulis et Circuli Linguistici Pragensis Sodalibus Oblata* (Prague, 1932).

Coleridge on Language

> ... it is the fundamental Mistake of Grammarians and Writers on the philosophy of Grammar and Language [to assume] that words and their syntaxis are the immediate representatives of Things, or that they correspond to Things. Words correspond to Thoughts; and the legitimate Order & Connection of words to the Laws of Thinking and to the acts and affections of the Thinker's mind.[29]

In order to establish his central concept of the linguistic sign, Saussure had to combat this same "fundamental Mistake," the notion that language is "a naming process only—a list of words each corresponding to the thing that it names." To neither the signifier nor the signified, the twin aspects of his linguistic sign, does he assign any referential function external to consciousness itself, *signifié* corresponding to a concept, not a thing. Though open to challenge in the extreme version of it elaborated by Roland Barthes and others, this doctrine has recently been adjudged "the most powerful assumption" in post-Saussurean French semiotics.[30] If so, the depth of Coleridge's insight deserves fuller appreciation than it has hitherto received.

Gerald L. Bruns also sees Coleridge as presaging structuralism in his anticipation of Saussure's rejection of the classical theory of correspondence for one conceived "diacritically in terms of the paradigmatic relations among words within a self-contained system." He even reads as an "approximate gloss" on Coleridge a key sentence in Claude Lévi-Strauss' *Structural Anthropology*: "The meaning of a word depends on the way in which language breaks up the realm of meaning to which the word belongs; and it is a function of the presence or absence of other

---

[29] *Letters*, VI, 630.
[30] *Course in General Linguistics*, trans. Wade Baskin (New York: McGraw-Hill, 1966), pp. 65, 66-67; Robert Scholes, "Toward a Semiotics of Literature," *Critical Inquiry*, IV (1977), 110.

words denoting related meanings." The often remarked seminal quality of Coleridge's thought, its almost infinite suggestiveness, may lead readers to ascribe to him more—or other—than his due. Bruns finds that the aphorism that "nothing can permanently please, which does not contain within itself the reason why it is so, and not otherwise," from the *Biographia*, Chapter XIV, foreshadows the Russian Formalist conception of *motivation*, according to which any element in a literary work is justified by its function in a structure, not to any external reference.[31] But Coleridge's sentence is demonstrably only an especially felicitous version of a central item of romantic literary organicism, not his exclusive discovery. He and Russian Formalism simply share a common ancestry on the point.

"Is thinking impossible," the young Coleridge had asked Godwin, "without arbitrary signs?" The answer supplied by his own later recorded observations clearly foreshadows Saussure's axiom that "our thought—apart from its expression in words—is only a shapeless and indistinct mass . . . a vague uncharted nebula." If Coleridge glimpsed any specific import for poetic theory in this virtual identity of intellection and verbalization, he seems never to have explored the question. We may suppose that here was one of the many hares started by his restless intellect not immediately pursued and thereafter lost sight of. On the other hand, the whole tenor of his linguistic thought harmonizes with the conviction of

---

[31] *Modern Poetry and the Idea of Language* (New Haven: Yale University Press, 1974), pp. 56-57, 94. Nonetheless, Bruns' discerning study is generally careful to avoid any simplistic conflation of structuralism and Coleridgean doctrine. He stresses the important difference that Coleridge's literary structure is "charged with energy: for him this 'breaking-up' of the realm of meaning belongs to the diachronic order of events, and not to the modern structuralist's world of purely formal or worldless systems." *Ibid.*, p. 57.

Coleridge on Language

the modern Formalist Jan Mukařovský that a sound poetics must recognize that "the *entire* realm of mental activity comprises a semantic structure. . . ."[32]

It should be stressed that Coleridge's assurance that language partook of its own vital, independent being never seduced him into the never-never land of *poésie pure*, as it might well have done. Poetry, he concedes, is something more than good sense, but it must be at least that, "just as a palace is more than a house, but . . . must be a house, at least."[33] Even when he is most enraptured by some specimen of verbal harmony (as, inevitably, by one of Shakespeare's) he is steadily aware that language, even the music of great verse, is not only never without some referential dimension, but that as T. S. Eliot cogently argues in "The Music of Poetry," its very musicality depends on ideation, "meaning" in some sense. This phenomenon (poorly grasped by my abstractions) Coleridge neatly encapsulated in a note on Hamlet's speech beginning "Seems, Madame?" (Act I, Scene 2). He calls attention to

the prodigality of beautiful words, which are, as it were, the half-embodyings of thoughts, that make them more than thoughts, give them an outness, a reality sui generis, *and yet retain their correspondence and shadowy approach to the images and movements within.*

Like other Shakespeareans since, he admits that in his earliest works the dramatist failed to effect the consummate harmony of music and meaning dis-

---

[32] *Course in General Linguistics*, pp. 111-112; Mukařovský, *The Word and Verbal Art: Selected Essays*, trans. and ed. John Burbank and Peter Steiner (New Haven: Yale University Press, 1977), pp. 59-60.

[33] *Table Talk* (New York: R. Worthington, 1884), p. 69. See also *Letters*, III, 470: "Poetry must be *more* than good sense, or it is not poetry; but it dare not be less, or discrepant."

played in *Hamlet* and the other mature plays. Nonetheless, Coleridge detects in the luxuriant verbal play of *Love's Labour's Lost* evidence of an overcharged mental energy venting itself in "lyric repetitions and sublime tautology"[34]—stylistic pecularities (we may note) located midway between the strict referentiality of prose and the conceptual nullity of music. In this respect, too, Coleridge is closer to most structuralist theory than to other formalisms (including certain distortions of formalist theory) which posit the aesthetic irrelevancy of intellectual content or communication in poetic expression. "Répétons-le une fois pour toutes," writes one structuralist: "la poésie est, comme la prose, un discours que l'auteur tient à son lecteur."[35]

It has been unfairly objected against all literary formalism whatever, typically by proponents of the biographical, sociological, and psychological schools of criticism, that it denies the cognitive element of poetry and even founds the value of poetic art precisely in the absence or irrelevance of that element. In fairness to the objectors, the intellectual purism of Edgar Poe's insistence that poetry can have only incidental relations with moral values or thought, or of Walter Pater's dictum that all art aspires to the condition of music, does give grounds for suspicion. What's more, in Poe's case at least, it would not be hard to show that his doctrine owes something to Coleridge's fundamental dichotomy of poetry and science. That Coleridge himself managed to avoid the heresy (to turn Poe's word against him) of his purist followers can in very large measure be credited to his unremit-

[34] *Shakespearean Criticism*, I, 35, 86-87 (emphasis mine).
[35] "Let us repeat it once for all; poetry, like prose, is speech which an author addresses to his reader." Jean Cohen, *Structure du langage poétique* (Paris: Flammarion, 1966), p. 182.

ting effort to penetrate the mystery of language in all its functions, nonaesthetic as well as aesthetic. Similarly, it is clear that the basic linguistic orientation of structuralist poetics has allowed its advocates to see that the superior expressiveness of poetic utterance inheres far less in a sensuous iconicity achieved through the traditional aural devices of alliteration, rhyme, and the rest, than in a referential and semantic intensity to which these are tributary.

How this intensity is effected is variously envisaged in structuralist speculation. Mukařovský notes that in verse alliteration, rhyme, and paronomasia themselves function semantically. Mikel Dufrenne perceives in the verbal ordonnance of verse a subordination of the syntactical to the lexical; and by this means, he argues, "la poésie augmente la quantité d'information." But whatever the specifics of their etiologies, they meet in the conviction that, as Archibald A. Hill quite simply puts it, "poetry always says something, indeed it says something more than what is said in ordinary language." But Coleridge's position perhaps finds its closest twentieth-century confirmation in a nonstructuralist stylistic critic, the late W. K. Wimsatt, who concluded that it is precisely "through being supercharged with significance" that a poem achieves aesthetic power.[36]

Of several conclusions about his account of poetic diction that may be drawn from Coleridge's life-long efforts to discover the laws of human utterance, one is especially relevant to our present concern. The dissent from Wordsworth's prefatorial strictures on po-

[36] Mukařovský, *The Word and Verbal Art*, p. 23; Dufrenne, *Le Poétique* (Paris: Presses Universitaires de France, 1973), p. 101; Hill, "Poetry and Stylistics," in *Essays on the Language of Literature*, p. 387; Wimsatt, *The Verbal Icon* (Lexington: University of Kentucky Press, 1954), p. 231.

etic style, and the theory offered in their stead which he elaborated in the second volume of *Biographia Literaria*, rest on a sustained study of the poet's medium surely unequaled by any critic before him. To a degree undeniable if not easily measured, this fact accounts for the enduring validity of the resultant theory itself, still in its essentials undiscredited by any other since advanced. The scores of observations on language and languages scattered throughout Coleridge's prose writings lend considerable force to Robert Scholes' declaration that his critiques of Wordsworth's and others' poetry "derive their authority from the strength of his linguistic grasp."[37]

But not immediately. The process evolves, rather, in three stages, an account of metrical language intervening between the general linguistics and the applied criticism. Coleridge thus fulfills, as already suggested, the requirement of the structuralist program which denies validity to any theory of poetic diction not based on a prior analysis of nonliterary speech. For the critic's first task, as an eminent structuralist has defined it, is to

connaître ce que sont les propriétés de la parole avant leur intégration dans une oeuvre. Cette étude préliminaire touchant les propriétés linguistiques des matériaux pré-litté-

[37] *Structuralism in Literature*, p. 179. Owen Barfield, whose opinion has the double authority of his being both a distinguished analyst of poetic language and a Coleridgean (see his *Poetic Diction* [1925] and *What Coleridge Thought* [1971]), has recently concluded that "it is perhaps because of such an intimate union of his own genius with the genius or spirit of language that his positive contributions to the thought of his age, and I would say of posterity, are so often to be found focused or concentrated in some particular word. And the same is true of those prophetic anticipations . . . of whole modes of thought which were later on to become part of the intellectual climate of every day." "Coleridge's Enjoyment of Words," in *Coleridge's Variety*, p. 214.

raires est necéssaire à la connaissance du discours littéraire lui-même. . . .[38]

The affinities between Coleridge's idea of poetic utterance and the discoveries of Jakobson and his fellows will perhaps seem less surprising when we recognize them as fruits of a shared duality of interest and approach. Russian formalist poetics, Gérard Genette has observed, has its origin in a meeting of linguists and critics on the shared terrain of poetic language.[39] In Coleridge's case the linguist and the critic inhabited the same skull.

That the best critics of the Victorian age, even those who revered Coleridge's memory (Arnold and Pater each wrote essays on him), were largely indifferent or purblind to his theoretical achievement is among the anomalies of intellectual history. Probably it is best explained by the fact that their energies were absorbed and their attention diverted by a different order of critical issues from those faced by writers of Coleridge's generation. Whatever the reasons, it was not until a century after his death that his poetics began to be properly appreciated. Only in the context of the rich flowering of twentieth-century criticism represented by the essays of T. S. Eliot and the theoretical speculations of the Slavic Formalists, I. A. Richards, the American New Criticism, and the newer structuralism, can we finally take the measure of its profundity and brilliance.

[38] ". . . understand what the properties of speech are before they are integrated into a literary work. This preliminary study of the linguistic properties of the preliterary materials is necessary for understanding literary discourse itself. . . ." Tzetvan Todorov, *Qu'est-ce que le Structuralisme?* pp. 39-40.

[39] Genette, *Figures I* (Paris: Editions du Seuil, 1966), p. 149.

II

The Language of Heaven

It is not hard to account for the note of barely restrained impatience audible in Coleridge's refutation of Wordsworth's notions of poetic language and form. In the Preface to *Lyrical Ballads* the almost casual dismissal of meter and related aspects of prosodic structure affronted Coleridge's dearest experiences as reader and poet as much as they clashed with his reasoned ideas about poetry. No aspect of the poet's art interested him more than its technique. Virgil, whose versification he admired "beyond measure," delighted him for that reason alone. To his rapt young audience at Highgate he complained of the neglect of versification by contemporary poets, among them Byron; and his chief impression of Tennyson's early work was that the young poet had begun to write verses without a proper understanding of meter![1]

In its hypersensitivity to metrical and rhythmical subtleties Coleridge's ear rivaled Pope's. Wordsworth is reported to have said that his friend blamed the paucity of his poetic output on the extreme care and labor he spent on his meters. "He said that when he was intent on a new experiment in metre, the time and labour he bestowed were inconceivable; that he was quite an epicure in sound." Coleridge contrasted

[1] *Letters*, II, 743; *Table Talk* (New York: R. Worthington, 1884), pp. 30, 32, 236.

the living poets' indifference to versification with the meticulous observance of it by Spenser in *Epithalamion*, "sometimes so extremely minute as to be painful even to my ear, and you know how highly I prize good versification."[2]

Highly indeed—enough to complain to Crabb Robinson of Wordsworth's carelessness with the mechanism of his verse; to name "perfect sweetness" of versification among the four symptoms of poetic power displayed by the young Shakespeare; to fill twenty consecutive pages of a notebook with passages from Italian and German poems only because they exemplified various meters and metrical effects; to plan a *Prosodia* (like Dryden's, never executed); to claim that he could determine the authenticity of a Shakespearean line by meter alone; to prize H. F. Cary's English *Divine Comedy* largely for its splendid blank verse, "the most various and harmonious . . . since Milton"; and to laud Mary Robinson's "Haunted Beach" exclusively for its metrical excellence: ". . . that Woman has an Ear."[3]

From the frequency and variety of his remarks on the craft we can infer something of the contents of the projected prosody, enough to regret that it was never written. The subject received the same multifaceted scrutiny that he directed to every other subject that stirred his intellect. He compares the several classical meters and their varying occurrence in English verse. He perceives the mimetic function of verse rhythm, especially in the drama. He finds the "very rhythm" of Lady Macbeth's speech of welcome to King Dun-

---

[2] Wordsworth is quoted in *The Complete Poetical Works of Samuel Taylor Coleridge*, ed. Hartley Coleridge, 2 vols. (London: Oxford University Press, 1912), II, 1014; *Table Talk*, p. 39.

[3] *Letters*, V, 261; *Biographia*, II, 14; *Notebooks*, II, note to entry 2224; *Shakespearean Criticism*, I, 123 n., 127 et passim; *Letters*, IV, 779; I, 576.

can a revelation of her insincerity. In William Sotheby's translation of Wieland's then popular *Oberon* he detects a metrical defect in its occasional pause at the second syllable of a line. Milton, Coleridge has noticed, never does this except to mark an unusual stress, and even then only with a trochaic foot, not a spondee or iamb. To blank verse he gives special attention, remarking on the rarity of the gift for executing it properly, "scarcely given to one in an age. . . ." With a nice aesthetic discrimination he separates genuine unrhymed iambic pentameter from the mere rhymeless or, in a telling epithet, "rhyme-craving" five-foot iambics too often produced, even by the admirable James Thomson. Blank verse, he instructs Southey, is a form that actually comprises five or six distinct meters—an insight that T. S. Eliot must surely have applauded.[4]

But the value Coleridge placed on metrical expression involved much more than a sensitivity to its pleasurable effects; he saw in it the ideal vehicle for embodying and inculcating the deepest truths. Years of reflection convinced him that "a true System of Philosophy . . . is *best* taught in Poetry as well as most safely," including the Truth of Christianity itself. In this regard we may ascribe to an identical conviction both his early hope that Wordsworth would write a great philosophical poem and his later stated intention, when in a deeply religious mood and only months from death, to produce a metrical translation of the *Apocalypse*.[5] To anyone so persuaded, Wordsworth's virtual conflation of prose and verse would seem not merely technically erroneous but well-nigh insensate.

Scriptural history, Coleridge wrote in *The States-*

[4] *Shakespearean Criticism*, I, 223, 66; *Letters*, III, 94, 71; IV, 782; III, 434.
[5] *Letters*, IV, 687; VI, 967.

man's Manual, presents us "the stream of time continuous as Life and a symbol of Eternity, inasmuch as the Past and the Future are virtually contained in the Present." I have elsewhere suggested that in place of his own wording of this elusive relation of time and eternity Coleridge might have preferred its metrical "celebration" in Eliot's "Burnt Norton":

Time present and time past
Are both perhaps present in time future
And time future contained in time past.

From scattered testimony by other poets through the ages one might conceivably put together a rationale for Coleridge's belief that certain subjects require metrical form for their proper verbalization. There is, for example, Pope's declaration that he chose verse rather than prose for expounding his ethical system (in *An Essay on Man*) because he found that verse made for a greater verbal economy. It would be too digressive to attempt here any explicit elaboration of a thesis only barely glimpsed in Coleridge's own writings. For the moment it will suffice to concede that there is nothing eccentric in his hunch (to set it no higher) that one ingredient of a sound definition of metrical discourse is its provision for the limitations of prose as a vehicle of communication. Any attentive reader of poetry may harbor the same suspicion. At least I am apparently not alone in sensing that certain passages in what many critics think the greatest poem in English of our century, *Four Quartets*, may be cases in point. In her fascinating recent account of the composition of that poem, Dame Helen Gardner cites the opinion of philosopher Donald MacKinnon, who finds in Part III of "Little Gidding" a "curious precision of language" in conveying its theme, a spiritual grasp of "the meaning of history."

If that phrase conveys anything, Dr. MacKinnon observed, "it may be the sort of thing that can only achieve its definition in poetry."[6] Such a conclusion, it is worth noting, would endow the traditional notion of "poetic ideas" with a new and less suspect import: thoughts not necessarily so lofty as to call for the dignity of verse but quite simply incommunicable in any other way.

Despite the fundamental difference in orientation between Wordsworth and Coleridge, on the question of poetic diction in its more limited sense their views had much in common, the Preface to *Lyrical Ballads* itself being, as Coleridge confessed to Southey, half his own brainchild. He fully shared Wordsworth's central objection to a poetic style too remote from the spoken idiom. In his dramatic poem *Osorio*, his avowed aim, expressed three years before the Preface to *Lyrical Ballads* appeared, was as far as possible to avoid sentences that might not be spoken in conversation, rejecting only those commonly so used. In 1802, the very year of the revised Preface, he mildly castigates Thomas Wedgwood for favoring in poetic diction an "aloofness" from real language, which he thinks "deadly to Poetry."[7]

In any modern assessment of Wordsworth's opinions about the poet's language we risk injustice by forgetting the immediate and practical necessities he faced as creative artist. Much of his distaste for the

[6] *The Collected Works of Samuel Taylor Coleridge*, ed. Kathleen Coburn (Princeton: Princeton University Press, 1969—), VI, *Lay Sermons*, ed. R. J. White (1972), p. 29. See my "T. S. Eliot and the Ghost of S.T.C.," *Sewanee Review*, LXXII (1964), 262-280; MacKinnon is quoted in Helen Gardner, *The Composition of Four Quartets* (London: Faber and Faber, 1978), pp. 210-211.

[7] *Letters*, II, 830; I, 356; II, 877. The danger of poetic "aloofness" from common speech, stressed by Dryden, Yeats, and Eliot, among the best poets, is of course virtually a truism of modern poetics.

"artificial" language of contemporary verse bespeaks his personal creative struggle against that burden of the past which Professor Bate has explored in its several fascinating and distressing ramifications. Poetic diction, whether one felt it as meretricious or beneficial, was by its very elegance and admitted efficacy in the most memorable poetry an obstacle to fresh composition. And so a portion of any young poet's creative effort had to be expended in trying to exorcise the seductive demon of this verbal heritage from his consciousness. With all but the most powerful and original talents the effort was doomed to failure because it was so fatally easy to sacrifice the integrity of one's vision by simply adapting it to some novel rearrangement of glittering locutions culled from the thesaurus of poetic tropes and figures. The only escape was to take refuge in a total renunciation of "poetic diction" and adopt instead the plainest possible style, because, as Coleridge could still complain over a dozen years after the liberating example of *Lyrical Ballads*,

it is scarcely practicable for a man to write in the ornamental style on any subject without finding his poem, against his will and without his previous consciousness, a cento of lines that had pre-existed in other works; and this it is which makes poetry so very difficult, because so very easy, in the present day. I myself have for many years past given it up in despair.[8]

He therefore had every sympathy with his friend's dilemma. What he could not endorse was Wordsworth's erecting his personal response to that dilemma into a theory that would not sustain rational examination.

[8] W. Jackson Bate, *The Burden of the Past and the English Poet* (Cambridge: Harvard University Press, 1970); *Letters*, III, 469-470.

No one has demonstrated more convincingly than Coleridge himself that the peculiar status of words in poetry cannot be understood except in relation to every other element of versification. Nonetheless, his scattered observations on poetic diction in the restricted sense of a choice of words suitable to poetry or to the context of a particular poem repay attention as so many glosses on the theory which he expounded in the *Biographia* and which he regarded as having settled the question as far as it lay within the wit of man to do. Surely a prime motive in his preoccupation with language, the subject is never far from his mind. Around the time of his departure for Malta in 1805 he copied into his notebook four of G. B. Marino's *Sonnetti* "for the sake of the Diction . . . my attention . . . being concentered and confined to this one Object while I am attempting to translate it."[9]

His penchant for savoring each word in a line of verse, sometimes challenging its place with a better, accords with that proviso in his celebrated definition of a poem that requires the pleasure from its totality to consist with a distinct gratification from the several parts. And in this regard it should be noted that the term *poetic diction* is too blunt for the precision of Coleridge's analysis, which apparently envisioned separate criteria of word choice corresponding to his discrimination of *poetry* from *poem*. Poems are subject to criteria of usage not binding upon poetry, broadly defined as the creation of the opposites-reconciling imagination, and often in the form of prose. Although the criteria governing this latter category are never explicitly formulated in his critical writings, he apparently assumed that he had made them sufficiently clear in the second volume of the *Biographia*, which, he assured Edward Coleridge in 1823, con-

---

[9] *Notebooks*, II, entry 2625.

tained "the true principles of judgement respecting Poetry, *Poem*, poetic & *poematic* Diction."[10] Whatever the accuracy of this claim, the theory I am examining here relates only to *poematic* diction, which in fact is the import the familiar term *poetic diction* still bears today: i.e., the language of metrical composition.

It's hardly possible to overstress the importance of verbal style in Coleridge's appraisals of poets and poems. He damns the stanza of Gray's ode on Eton College beginning "Say, Father Thames" as the worst ten lines in Gray's whole work, verse and prose, English and Latin, simply because they are "very objectionable in point of diction." Reviewing his own juvenilia, he is abashed at their "general turgidness of diction," just as he lists the opposite virtue, a "frequent curiosa felicitas of his diction," among several characteristic excellences of Wordsworth's poetry. In keeping with the cast of his theory-prone intellect, most of Coleridge's references to poetic style exemplify some general principle or problem. How, for instance, avoid bathos (or worse) when giving expression to the vulgar or the commonplace? Shakespeare—than whom Addison himself, he asserts, took no more care to be "poetical in diction,"—in a passage in *Hamlet* shows every young poet *"how* to elevate a thing almost mean by its familiarity":

I have heard
The cock, that is the trumpet to the morn,
Doth with his lofty and shrill-sounding throat
Awake the god of day.[11]

[10] *Letters*, V, 287.
[11] *Coleridge's Miscellaneous Criticism*, ed. Thomas Middleton Raysor (Cambridge: Harvard University Press, 1936), p. 307 (hereafter cited as *Miscellaneous Criticism*); *Biographia*, I, 2; II, 121; *Shakespearean Criticism*, I, 19.

Coleridge's study of Shakespeare led him to speculate as well on the special problems of poetry in the theater. He distinguishes poetic from dramatic speech, which he thinks Shakespeare himself at first confused. In *Romeo and Juliet*, for example, Capulet and Montague sometimes sound like poets talking, a fault finally overcome in Shakespeare's later masterpieces but which many lesser dramatists were to commit throughout their careers. This distinction is related to the pre-Romantic doctrine of generic styles, which retains force in Coleridge's thought. To August Wilhelm Schlegel's observation that the pompous style of the player's dramatic recitation in *Hamlet* appropriately sets it off from the rest of the blank verse, mimetic of real speech, Coleridge shrewdly adds that the player's speech is in the necessarily more elevated epic style.[12]

But what in fact constitutes the difference between the styles of lyric (or epic) and dramatic verse? This Coleridge was never able clearly to elucidate, although like many others equally baffled he was fully sensible of the difference between them in practice. A note on Francisco's remark, "Not a mouse stirring," from *Hamlet*, I, i, reveals at once his intense interest in the question and his failure to articulate a solution. This remark, he wrote, has

its dramatic use and purpose, for its commonness in ordinary conversation tends to produce the sense of reality, and at once hides the poet and yet approximates the reader or spectator to that state in which the highest poetry will appear, and in its component parts, tho' not in the whole composition, really is the language of nature. If I should not speak it, I feel that I should be thinking it; the voice only is the poet's, the words are my own.[13]

[12] *Shakespearean Criticism*, II, 102; I, 37.
[13] *Ibid.*, I, 38-39.

The Language of Heaven

It would be hard to find in all of Coleridge's prose a passage more tantalizing for its combination of suggestiveness and obscurity; one feels that in this case he was simply unable to express what he had not clearly conceived. If so, we should reflect that the issue he faced is among the most elusive in poetics. T. S. Eliot, it is instructive to recall, grappled with it early and late in his critical essays, without arriving at a firm solution. His ambition to write excellent yet popular verse plays led him to put the question in the most practical terms: how to write genuine verse for the stage which, when spoken by actors, would not give the impression of people "talking poetry."[14] His modest confession that he never quite succeeded in doing so should make us hesitate to judge Coleridge too severely for failing to attain a firm grasp of the relevant theory.

Romantic though he was, at least by chronology, Coleridge never confused good poetic usage with flowery language. It may not be truistic to insist on this fact in view of a passage every reader of the *Biographia* will readily recall. He first presents, in a succinct couplet, a description of trees agitated by a sea breeze:

Behold yon row of pines, that shorn and bow'd
Bend from the sea-blast, seen at twilight eve,

and then observes that the same image becomes more poetic when rewritten thus:

Yon row of bleak and visionary pines,
By twilight glimpse discerned, mark! how they flee
From the fierce sea-blast, all their tresses wild
Streaming before them.

---

[14] See his essays on "Poetry and Drama" and "The Three Voices of Poetry" in *On Poetry and Poets*.

He is concerned here only to show that good poetry is more than an accurate description of nature: there must also be an infusion of the poet's own intellectual and affective being. But the illustration, of his own devising, seems rather to exalt verbal elaboration for its own sake. His taste, however, was if anything for the opposite, so much so that we can readily imagine his endorsing—and *understanding*—Ezra Pound's aphorism that poetry ought to be as well written as prose. Equally in both forms he was a stickler for semantic precision, which to him embraced not alone the denotation of a word but the whole range of its connotative overtones as well. He once scolded Southey for writing in one poem that a gibbet "engages" the eye, because the related form *engaging* carries the connotation of pleasing.[15]

Of course no one is likely to accuse the author of *The Rime of the Ancient Mariner* of a hankering after pedestrian phraseology in verse. Yet it is true that Coleridge's taste favored an eloquence of the simple and direct (*not* the prosaic) over the ornate. In the *Biographia* he is pleased to recall his preference for the "natural language" of "I will remember thee" to the "ragtag finery" of

Thy image on her wing
Before my FANCY's *eye shall* MEMORY *bring.*

He relished the "pure, manly, unaffected" diction of George Herbert's poems. *The Flower*, in which Herbert wrote, "I once more smell the dew and rain, And relish versing," was a special favorite. "And relish versing," he told the artist William Collins, conveys sincerity and reality far better than the more

---

[15] *Biographia*, II, 17; *Letters*, I, 334.

The Language of Heaven

"dignified" style of "and once more love the Muses" could do.[16]

Coleridge liked to define prose as words in their best order and poetry as the best words in the best order. Since he thought well of these "homely definitions" and commended them to aspiring poets, it seems useful to fix their meaning, especially the precise import of those unspecified "best words." The evidence that this phrase has no reference to anything like the figment of an exclusively poetic vocabulary is too well acknowledged to need citation. If, equally, we cannot derive from anywhere in Coleridge's writings a definition in form of "best words," he does at least provide a test for detecting their presence or absence in any given poem. When, some years ago, I mistook as an original personal discovery the idea that in poetry there are, strictly speaking, no synonyms, I had forgotten one of the two critical aphorisms on poetic style offered in the first chapter of *Biographia Literaria*: "that whatever lines can be translated into other words of the same language, without diminution of their significance . . . are so far vicious in their diction."[17]

[16] *Biographia*, I, 13-14; *The Friend*, I, 45; *Letters*, IV, 893. In this same letter to Collins, of December 1818, he confesses that earlier in life he used to laugh at Herbert's quaint style. One hopes that his "emendation" of the delicious image in "Virtue," "A box where sweets compacted lie" to "A *nest* where sweets compacted lie" belongs to this earlier time. But it is so quoted in the *Biographia*. See also *Miscellaneous Criticism*, p. 246.

[17] *Table Talk*, p. 48; *Biographia*, I, 14. In view of Coleridge's admiration for the homogeneous languages noted above, his concession that "composite" English is a "happier instrument of expression" than homogeneous German, incapable of such richness as "the pomp and prodigality of Heaven," is noteworthy. But he is careful to label Shakespeare's alliterated nouns Saxon and Latin "quasi-synonymes," not synonyms proper. *Table Talk*, pp. 198-199.

The Language of Heaven

This way of putting it may seem too exacting, demanding an ideal almost impossible of attainment. Nonetheless, that Coleridge seriously intended this formula as a norm, even while he recognized the virtual impossibility of its fulfillment in practice, is made evident by a later passage in the book. Because it so succinctly clenches the conclusion of all his prior thought on the subject, I quote at length.

In poetry, in which every line, every phrase, may pass the ordeal of deliberation and deliberate choice, it is possible, and barely possible, to attain that ultimatum which I have ventured to propose as the infallible test of a blameless style; its untranslatableness *in words of the same language without injury to the meaning. Be it observed, however, that I include in the* meaning *of a word not only its correspondent object, but likewise all the associations which it recalls. For language is framed to convey not the object alone, but likewise the character, mood and intentions of the person who is representing it.*

In contrast to the prose-writer, the poet can preserve his diction from corruption by the contagion of promiscuous scribbling. "Yet even to the poet," he continues,

composing in his own province, it is an arduous work: and as the result and pledge of a watchful good sense, of fine and luminous distinction, and of complete self-possession, may justly claim all the honor which belongs to an attainment equally difficult and valuable, and the more valuable for being rare. It is at all *times the proper food of the understanding; but in an age of corrupt eloquence it is both food and antidote.* [18]

[18] *Biographia,* II, 115-116.

This passage serves notice that the poet who can successfully fulfill the social role of preserving the idiom, which Dante, Coleridge, and Eliot assign him, must combine the virtues of hero and saint. But to assess its full import for the problem of poetic language it must be set in the context of similar references to the creative agony that is experienced, alone among artists, by the craftsman in words. It is Coleridge's most emphatic version of Pope's boast that the best poets are those who have the guts to "show no mercy to an empty line"; or of Keats' self-punishing effort (commended to Shelley) to load every rift with ore, a work harder, as W. B. Yeats sang of it in "Adam's Curse," than an old pauper's breaking stones. But in his recognition that a command of what he honored as "the language of heaven" has been made more arduous by the leveling down of literacy, Coleridge's version is closest to Eliot's arresting testimony to the twentieth-century poet's intolerable wrestle with words in conditions no longer propitious. Theorists of poetic diction can hardly be blamed for slighting this aspect of the question since it belongs to the indeterminate element of individual genius, for which, almost by definition, no theory can account. Still, it is well to be reminded—and it is always by those poets who combine a supreme degree of the creative gift with unusual critical acumen—that the stuff of our theorizing is no natural boon but a treasure dearly won.

III

The Universal Principle

Of Wordsworth's declarations that the language of good poetry is ideally derived from rustic speech, and that there is no essential difference between the languages of poetry and prose, Coleridge provided the readers of the *Biographia Literaria* with a bi-level refutation. On the first level, which has received the bulk of critical attention since, are several more or less direct denials of these assertions themselves or of assumptions they seem to entail. Thus he retorts that the best part of any language comes not from the countryman's daily communion with nature but from the intellectual and imaginative activity of educated minds; and that the essential disparity of the styles of prose and verse is enforced by the agency of meter in the latter. By an appeal to common observation, he effectively challenges the Rousseauistic primitivism of Wordsworth's faith in the moral superiority of rural life and, consequently, of rustic speech. And so on.[1]

Leaving these and similar observations aside, I would stress instead the more fundamental level of Coleridge's counterargument, his distinction between a copy and an imitation, because upon this distinction his own theory of verse language centrally rests. Disregard or misconception of this principle makes impossible any clear understanding of the the-

[1] See *Biographia*, Chapters XVII and XVIII *passim*.

The Universal Principle

ory itself, let alone the justice of Coleridge's faith that human reason could devise none better.

Since students of Coleridge's literary theory have paid little attention to the concept, I ought perhaps to point out that my own high estimate of its importance has the warrant of Coleridge himself. Beyond its citation at crucial points of his theoretical arguments, there is his explicit declaration that the distinction between a copy and an imitation is no less than "the universal principle of the fine arts."[2] That such was his settled conviction is borne out not only by the fact that he applies it to the drama, opera, painting, sculpture, and acting, as well as to poetry; it is further supported by the close logical relation of an imitation, as he defines it, to such other major principles of his aesthetic as "multëity in unity" (i.e. beauty) and the polar action of the creative imagination. The fatal flaw in Wordsworth's theory of poetic language lay in his substituting a copy for a true imitation, which is tantamount to a misconception of artistic mimesis. His adoption of the real language of men would yield little more than a reproduction of human speech. His equation of prose and verse failed to recognize that the two kinds of verbal expression belong to two generically disparate modes of relation to perceived reality, which Coleridge found it historically convenient to denominate respectively *copy* and *imitation*. Prose, here meaning nonfictional discourse, since it aspires to an objective rendering of experiential reality or (as in philosophic or scientific writing) of conceptual truth, could with no disparagement be labeled a copy of nature (though all but the barest notation is rather more than that). Verse, however, which inevitably subjected the reality it represented to various formal distortions and patternings as a

[2] *Shakespearean Criticism*, I, 181.

condition of attaining aesthetic quality, was fittingly called a mode of imitation. Fittingly, because the word is the Latin-derived equivalent of the Greek *mimesis*, which in the *Poetics* Aristotle defines precisely in terms of its radical difference from that mirrorlike mimicry of the sensible world to which Plato had reduced the poet's mimetic function in his *Republic*. Although essentially, then, Coleridge's conception is Aristotelian and hence traditional, his contribution to its further exposition is vital, both as a general aesthetic principle and in its specific bearing on poetic theory. By redefining artistic imitation to consist with his aesthetic of polar opposites, he developed a mimetic analysis of poetic language that is, I think, salutary. It avoids the impasses and contradictions of all previous speculation and bears comparison with the most cogent modern prosody.

This is not to say that most modern prosodic analysis is explicitly mimetic. Nonetheless, Northrop Frye, whose critical theory, so different in other respects, accords with J. C. Ransom's belief that the doctrine of mimesis "is probably the best foundation for any aesthetic," always assumes or asserts a mimetic relation in his many references to fictional and poetic discourse. Even the style of so-called conversational poetry, he notes, "is not that of ordinary speech, but a special literary imitation of it. . . ." More recently Barbara H. Smith has skillfully defended the thesis that a poem is not an utterance but an imitation of an utterance.[3]

The fact that in the long history of mimetic theory since Aristotle *copy* and *imitation* often served as alter-

---

[3] Ransom, *The World's Body* (New York: Scribner's, 1930), p. 197; Frye, *The Well-Tempered Critic* (Bloomington: Indiana University Press, 1963), p. 68; Smith, "Poetry as Fiction," *New Literary History*, II (1971), 259-281. See also her *Poetic Closure* (Chicago: University of Chicago Press, 1968).

The Universal Principle

nate designations of the same phenomenon reminds us that in opposing one to the other Coleridge is being faithful to his own maxim that intellectual advance consists in desynonymization. Two notebook entries vie for the honor of being his first mention of the opposition. One of these, applying it to stage plays and the opera, Miss Coburn refers to 1805. To the other entry, which he printed in *Anima Poetae*, E. H. Coleridge assigned the date of 1804, followed in this by Shawcross. Conceding this date to be probably correct, Miss Coburn nonetheless presents other evidence that this entry may have been recorded as late as 1808.[4]

I allude to the dating of these notes because it relates to a question best disposed of before proceeding further in analysis: what degree of originality may Coleridge claim for his separation of copy from imitation? Do we have here another instance of his borrowing an idea without acknowledgment from some prior expositor, German or other? The dates of these earliest references to it would seem of themselves effectively to refute the notion that Coleridge owed the concept to Friedrich Schelling, because that philosopher's *Philosophische Schriften*, which Coleridge certainly saw and from which he borrowed other materials in close paraphrase, was not published until 1809. Nonetheless, since despite years of exhaustive debate the nature and extent of Coleridge's dependence on German sources remain in question, the best way to clarify the limited aspect of it that concerns us here is by a direct comparison of the relevant passages.

First the two pre-Schelling notebook entries. The first one clearly shows Coleridge noticing the phe-

[4] *Notebooks*, II, entry 2211 and note; entry 2274 and note; *Anima Poetae*, ed. Ernest Hartley Coleridge (Boston: Houghton-Mifflin, 1895), p. 74; *Biographia*, II, 273.

The Universal Principle

nomenon and confessing some difficulty in grasping its etiology:

Hard to express that sense of the analogy or likeness of a Thing which enables a Symbol to represent it, so that we think of the Thing itself—& yet knowing that the Thing is not present to us. —Surely, on this universal fact of words & images depends by more or less mediations the imitation instead of copy which is illustrated in very nature shakespearianized—that Proteus Essence that could assume the very form, but yet known & felt not to be the Thing by that difference of the Substance which made every atom of the Form another thing—that likeness not identity—an exact web, every line of direction miraculously the same, but the one worsted, the other silk. [5]

Except for the happy introduction of the antithetical terms themselves, all we have here so far is an unusually subtle expression of the age-old mystery of mimetic art that may be conveniently reduced to a series of paradoxes: first, how a segment of experience (*alias* life, nature, reality) can be recognizably represented in a medium, words or pigments, totally alien to the stuff of the original; second, why that reproduction takes on a value not discernible in the original; third—and most puzzling—why that value seems to depend on the degree (within limits) to which the representation avoids *exact* reproduction. All this had been noticed, and noted, before, as it has been since, by other creative writers as well as by aestheticians. In a portrait, John Dryden discovered, there may be too great a likeness to the subject, just as he punctured Robert Howard's fallacious dramatic realism by pointing to the radical difference between the real Bartholemew Fair and Ben Jonson's comedy so named. The one, Dryden remarked, is "vile," the

[5] *Notebooks*, II, entry 2274.

The Universal Principle

other "of price," fair alternates to Coleridge's image of worsted and silk.[6]

The second pre-Schelling notebook entry also makes no attempt at resolving these paradoxes, but it does offer a sound application of the "universal principle" to the opera. Objections to its unreality, Coleridge points out, rest on the false assumption that it is a copy of nature, whereas a musical drama, like a play, is an imitation of nature.[7]

Given these prior observations of his own, Coleridge must certainly have been more than casually interested when he came on Schelling's censure of artists who "reproduce the existent with servile fidelity" and therefore "produce masks, but no works of art." Schelling, too, poses the familiar problem. "How does it come about, he asks,

that, to everyone whose taste is to some degree educated, imitations of the real which are pushed to the point of illusion appear in the highest degree unreal, making, indeed, the impression of spectres, whereas a work in which the idea is regnant strikes every such observer with the full force of truth and actually transports him for the first time into the genuinely real world?[8]

Admittedly Schelling's question refers to the same phenomenon from which Coleridge's speculation starts—the repulsiveness of photographic realism. But there the similarity between them ends. The German's formulation of the problem is not Coleridge's: that slavish imitation is false whereas genuine art reveals the idea ("Begriff") which alone is the essential

---

[6] *Essays of John Dryden*, ed. W. P. Ker, 2 vols. (Oxford: The Clarendon Press, 1900), I, 114, 115.

[7] *Notebooks*, II, entry 2211.

[8] "Concerning the Relation of the Plastic Arts to Nature," trans. Michael Bullock in Herbert Read, *The True Voice of Feeling* (New York: Pantheon, 1953), pp. 332, 333.

truth. His somewhat tautological "solution" departs even further from Coleridge's: that the beholder resents the absence of the idea, the only "living element" in nature, all else being unreal and empty shadows. Nor does Schelling oppose to the deceptive copy ("die bis zur Täuschung betriebenen Nachahmung") any polar term for the valid mimesis. Most important, both his statement of the problem and his solution are idealist and epistemological, whereas, for all his own idealist orientation and his faith in the cognitive value of poetry, Coleridge's formulation is fundamentally empirical and psychological. In a word, on this issue Schelling is Platonic, or neo-Platonic; Coleridge, essentially, Aristotelian.

This attribution may seem doubtful to those who recall that Coleridge, positing a temperamental dichotomy of humanity into Platonists and Aristotelians, enrolled himself enthusiastically among the former. But I am not alone in arguing the fundamentally Aristotelian cast of his mimetic theory. Long ago T. M. Raysor perceived that Coleridge's *copy* and *imitation* parallel the Platonic and Aristotelian views of poetic imitation. Among current scholars, Owen Barfield has conceded that the critical principles Coleridge actually applies in the chapters devoted to poetic diction in the *Biographia* echo those of Aristotle and Dr. Johnson. It is also notable that in that very section of the *Biographia* Coleridge's notion of the ideal as it is expressed in poetry is not Platonic or neo-Platonic but explicitly Aristotelian. "I adopt with full faith the principle of Aristotle, that poetry as poetry is essentially *ideal*. . . ."[9]

The contrasting ideas of mimesis held by the German thinker and his English admirer appear in the

[9] Raysor, *Shakespearean Criticism*, I, 177 n.; Barfield, *What Coleridge Thought* (Middletown, Conn.: Wesleyan University Press, 1971), p. 73; *Biographia*, II, 33. See also Walter Jackson Bate, *Coleridge* (New York: Macmillan, 1968), p. 164.

very essay, "On Poesy or Art," which is made up in great part of distressingly close paraphrases of Schelling's oration "Concerning the Relation of the Plastic Arts to Nature," from which the quotations above are taken, eked out by hints from the same author's *Transcendental Idealism*. In every true imitation, as distinct from a copy, Coleridge argues,

two elements must coexist, and not only coexist, but must be perceived as coexisting. These two elements are likeness and unlikeness, or sameness and difference, and in all genuine creations of art there must be a union of these disparates. The artist may take his point of view where he pleases, provided that the desired effect be perceptibly produced,— that there be likeness in the difference, difference in the likeness, and a reconcilement of both in one.

This account is perfectly consistent with every other reference Coleridge makes to copy-vs.-imitation and equally foreign to Schelling. So with his explanation of the repulsiveness of *trompe-l'oeil* art, which immediately follows:

If there be likeness to nature without any check of difference, the result is disgusting, and the more complete the delusion, the more loathsome the effect. Why are such simulations of nature, as waxwork figures of men and women, so disagreeable? Because, not finding the motion and the life which we expected, we are shocked as by a falsehood, every circumstance of detail, which before induced us to be interested, making the distance from truth more palpable. You set out with a supposed reality and are disappointed and disgusted with the deception; whilst in respect to a work of genuine imitation, you begin with an acknowledged total difference, and then every touch of nature gives you the pleasure of an approximation to truth. [10]

[10] *Biographia*, II, 256.

One can therefore endorse G.N.G. Orsini's statement[11] that the distinction between a copy and an imitation was one of Coleridge's original additions to the otherwise largely Schellingian material of "On Poesy or Art" only with the reservations that it is expressed and significantly illustrated independently of Schelling, and that its terms are ill-suited to those of Schelling's system.

On the other hand, as with every other idea since the Fall, Coleridge's originality does not preclude all intellectual ancestry. Condemnations of slavish copying of reality are a staple of Western criticism, beginning with Aristotle's ban on what he calls unity of the hero. Some Coleridgeans have seen a source for his idea in Plotinus, who in the Eighth Tractate of the fifth *Ennead* defended the artists' imitations because "they give no bare reproduction of the thing seen" but imbue their works with ideal elements drawn from their own souls.[12] But this conception bears so tenuous a relation to Coleridge's line of reasoning that we can hardly suppose his theory would have been other than it is had he never heard of the *Enneads*. The same may be said for J. J. Winckelmann's similar view that admirers and imitators of Greek sculpture always find in it something more than natural beauty, namely "gewisse idealische Schönheiten." Another passage in this same treatise on modern imitation of classical painting and sculpture, published in 1755, bears an initially deceptive resemblance to Coleridge because it exalts one kind of imitation ("Nachahmung") over another which he labels

[11] In *Coleridge and German Idealism* (Carbondale, Ill.: Southern Illinois University Press, 1969), p. 229.

[12] *The Enneads*, trans. Stephen MacKenna, 4th ed. rev. by B. S. Page (New York: Random House, 1969), pp. 422-423. J. Shawcross and I. A. Richards cite Plotinus as a source for Coleridge's idea. See *Biographia*, II, 318 and *Coleridge on Imagination* (London: Routledge and Kegan Paul, 1950), pp. 26-27.

The Universal Principle

a resembling copy ("eine ähnliche Kopie"). But Winckelmann's *Kopie* is only the less valuable of two quite legitimate ways of representing natural beauty in art. The "copyist," by rather naively reproducing a single attractive feature of the reality, produces mere portraits, by the method that yields Dutch forms and figures ("der Weg zum holländischen Formen und Figuren"). The Greek sculptors took the better way, creating out of many beautiful features, severally observed, the universal beauty of an ideal form. In Winckelmann, it is clear, the two terms are employed only for the polemical purpose of exalting classical art at the expense of modern modes. He departs even further from Coleridge when he accounts for the Greeks' superior achievement by their daily opportunity to observe natural beauty ("durch eine tägliche Gelegenheit zur Beobachtung des Schönen der Natur"). Throughout his critical writing Coleridge emphatically asserts that successful artistic rendering of reality is not a product of observation but a work of the imagination. Henry James' denial that any more than the slightest personal experience is required for convincing fictional treatment of a given subject would have been no news to the critic who told his lecture audiences that Shakespeare did not form the image of Dogberry, that ludicrous quintessence of the stupid constable, by studying dumb cops in real life.[13]

Since he never mentions Winckelmann, it is possible that Coleridge either did not know his work or was little impressed by it. But he did admire Joshua Reynolds' *Discourses on Art*, and in number thirteen

---

[13] Johann Joachim Winckelmann, "Gedanken über die Nachahmung der Griecheschen Werke in der Malerei und Bildhauerkunst," in *Winckelmanns Werke in Einem Band* (Berlin: Aufbau Verlag, 1969), pp. 3, 11. Compare James's views in "The Art of Fiction" with Coleridge's in *Shakespearean Criticism*, II, 218.

he would have found expressed two notions at least supportive of his own view of the relation of reality and art. Reynolds denied that painting was an imitation "operating by deception." Like Coleridge, Reynolds also insisted on the artificiality of poetic style, always "a violation of common speech" irrespective of its particular meter, historical period, or language. But Coleridge could have found no encouragement for his own line of throught in the famous painter's further observation that his art was "no imitation at all of external nature." Though Sir Joshua's notions would certainly have struck him as sounder than those of most eighteenth-century writers, there is no evidence to suppose they did more than confirm some part of his independently formed convictions on the matter. Coleridge may have taken the waxwork figure as an example of disagreeable realism from Reynolds, who uses it for exactly that purpose in the eleventh *Discourse*. Mere "copiers," the fabricators of these creations, he instructs the graduates of the Royal Academy, are not to be classed with painters of genius. But Coleridge does not follow him in ascribing our pleasure in fine painting simply to "seeing ends accomplished by seemingly inadequate means."[14]

Two other eighteenth-century thinkers whom Coleridge certainly read, the German Moses Mendelssohn and the Scotsman Adam Smith, may equally well have supplied Coleridge with both of his apt illustrations of tasteless mimicry: waxwork and artificial garden products. In the "Rhapsodie, oder Zusätze zu den Briefen über Empfindungen," included in his *Philosophische Schriften* (1761), Mendelssohn joined the long list of decriers of deceptive rep-

[14] *Discourses on Art*, ed. Robert R. Wark (San Marino, Cal.: Huntington Library, 1959), pp. 232, 234, 193.

The Universal Principle

resentation in art. His examples are painted statues and wax simulacra of men and women, life-sized and dressed in real clothing. Smith too, in an essay on imitation in the fine arts published in a posthumous collection of his writings in 1795, condemned both painted statues and "the works of Mrs. Wright" as types of repulsive imitation. The latter reference is undoubtedly to the American-born Patience Wright, who moved to London in 1772 and opened a waxwork exhibit there. Dubbed the "Promethean Modeller," she was celebrated for the striking realism of her clothed, life-sized figures of notable contemporaries, including one of Lord Chatham which still exists. Though in one of his many references to objectionable copies in art Coleridge pointedly names Smith's essays as source, he never alludes to Mendelssohn in this connection. Yet it seems highly likely that on one or two occasions he had the German thinker in mind as well, if only in unconscious recollection, because his chief objection to these delusive fabrications, our shock of disappointment at not finding life and motion in them, paraphrases Mendelssohn's: "so vermissen wir mit Widerwillen das Kenzeichen des Lebens, die Bewegung." And in another of the *Philosophische Schriften* pieces, "Ueber die Hauptgrundsätze der Schönen Künste und Wissenschaften," Mendelssohn contrasts a rose as admirably painted in a still-life by Van Huysum with one cast in metal or glass designed to look like the real thing.[15] In one of his letters quoted below (IV, 62-63), Cole-

---

[15] Mendelssohn, *Gesammelte Schriften. Jubiläumsausgabe* (Stuttgart: Friedrich Frommann Verlag, 1971—), I, 391-392; 433; Smith, "Of the Nature of That Imitation Which Takes Place in What Are Called the Imitative Arts," in *Early Writings of Adam Smith*, ed. J. Ralph Lindgren (New York: Augustus M. Kelley, 1967), p. 141. I am indebted to Professor René Wellek for calling the passages in Mendelssohn to my attention.

ridge ranks this same painter's fruitpieces among genuine imitations, in a judgment that relegates marble peaches to the reviled status of copies.

Nonetheless, as with Schelling's argument for the aesthetic poverty of a facsimile, Coleridge's rationale is otherwise totally discrepant from Mendelssohn's. Their differences appear at the very outset of his account as stated in the "Hauptgrundsätze." Whereas Coleridge condemns *any* reproduction aiming at an exact duplication of a natural original as constituting an "idle rivalry" with nature itself, Mendelssohn accords a certain minimal degree of pleasure-giving quality to this kind of product, figures done in plaster of Paris, for example. The reasons he adduces for the greater value of imitations that perceptibly differ from their originals have little or nothing in common with those of Coleridge. One of them closely parallels Plotinus in ascribing such artistic value to the beholder's perception of the artist's soul in his work. A second argument reiterates Winckelmann's doctrine that the art work embodies a transcendent ideal beauty by bringing into concentrated unity several "beauties" widely scattered in nature. As we shall see below, all this is irrelevant to the dynamic organicism of likeness and difference expounded in Coleridge's mimetic theory. Least of all, despite his own deeply religious intellectual orientation, would Coleridge have found anything to the purpose in the disconcerting shift from aesthetics to piety in Mendelssohn's version of the familiar analogy between the artist and God. Our delight in natural beauty, he finds, is "enkindled to rapture" ("bis zur Entzückung angefeuert") when seen as reflecting the infinite perfection of the Almighty. An atheist must therefore content himself with the much lower kind of pleasure afforded by the objects themselves.[16] Although there

---

[16] *Biographia*, II, 257; Mendelssohn, *Gesammelte Schriften*, I, 433-435.

The Universal Principle

is nothing in Coleridge's writings to suggest that he would have quarreled with this reflection taken by itself, it is nevertheless hard to imagine any line of reasoning less compatible with his thinking than so bald a confounding of pious contemplation and aesthetic experience.

Though here one is admittedly in the realm of conjecture, it seems fair to conclude that if either of these earlier writers was of any material use to Coleridge in working out his mimetic theory, it was the one he himself cites. In one of the most enlightening illustrations of the principle, he applies it to the contrasting effects of stage scenery and landscape painting. Like the wax effigy or a marble peach on a mantle, a mere copy of reality, stage scenery aims at delusion; the painting, an imitation, does not. Whether or not we ever *are* deluded in either case, with the painting "it is a *condition* of all genuine delight, that we should *not* be deluded. See *Adam Smith's Posthumous Essays.*" Smith, be it noted, is evoked chiefly to support the point that mimicry is repulsive in art. His illustrations, apparently by easy coincidence, are precisely those offered by Mendelssohn. We cannot pardon artificial fruits and flowers, he observes in the work to which Coleridge draws our attention, for lacking freshness and flavor, whereas we never weary of a good painting of these products of the garden. But he makes the further and more fundamental point, which, as is apparent in the passage quoted above from "On Poesy or Art," also forms a part of Coleridge's explanation: that in all good imitation there must be a perceived difference between the work and the object it imitates. Thus, Smith concludes, painting excells sculpture because of the disparity between its two-dimensional medium and the tridimensional form of real objects.[17]

[17] *Shakespearean Criticism*, I, 177; Smith, *Early Writings*, pp. 142, 139.

Yet even in the case of Smith the discrepancies between him and Coleridge easily outweigh the points of likeness. For one, nowhere does Smith use the term *copy* as opposed to *imitation*. More important, no more than Mendelssohn does he see any positive aesthetic value in the mimetic disparity he desiderates, his pleasure arising mainly from a recognition of the artist's skill in mastering material so recalcitrant to replication. Although he concedes that song enhances its mimetic objects (discourse and sentiment) through melody and harmony, he does not find that statuary and painting add any new beauties of their own to those of the nature they imitate.[18] Coleridge's profound experience to the contrary was in fact the chief *raison d'être* of his desynonymization of these two primary items in the terminology of traditional mimetic thought. As with all sound theory, the experience came first, in this instance the miracle-like conversion of nature's worsted into the silk of art.

Before exploring the central place copy-vs.-imitation holds in Coleridge's discussion of poetic language, it may be well to take note of certain misconstructions (as I take them to be) of his mimetic theory by some recent commentators. In his fine study of Coleridge and German idealist thought, G.N.G. Orsini declares that both copy and imitation, as Coleridge conceives them, deny the artist's creativity. "They have in common the reference to an external object on one side, and on the other the lack of reference to the creative power of the artist." More recently, from the broader perspective of a difference between neoclassical mimesis, founded on the belief in an orderly cosmos analogized in the art work, and Romantic expressionism consequent on the attenuation of that belief, Murray Krieger has virtually de-

---

[18] Smith, *Early Writings*, p. 156.

nied any place to mimesis in Coleridge's literary thought. His concept of the imagination, Krieger declares, simply replaces mimetic with expressionist theory.[19]

However valid Krieger's position may be as an historical generalization, neither it nor Orsini's stricture holds true of Coleridge himself. Krieger's conclusion requires no more refutation than that provided by the several passages from Coleridge's writings already cited, which show his idea of the creative imagination to be not an abandonment of mimesis but a radically corrective refinement of earlier and cruder versions of it. These same citations also make it hard to accept Orsini's alleged denial of creativity. Beyond the contrary import of their content, however, is an observation in the *Biographia* sufficient of itself to justify a conclusion directly opposite to Orsini's. Coleridge speaks there of the naturalness of Wordsworth's representations of rustic life, "as raised and qualified by an imperceptible infusion of the author's own knowledge and talent, which infusion does, indeed, constitute it an *imitation* as distinguished from a mere *copy*."[20] Coleridge's imitation is precisely a manifestation of the poet's creative manipulation of the life-stuff that constitutes the materials of his poem.

A more telling critique of Coleridge's distinction of terms appears in J. A. Appleyard's *Coleridge's Philosophy of Literature*. Father Appleyard is surely right that the phraseology of Coleridge's explanation is sometimes less than clear, and his own attempts to clarify its meaning do much to prevent misreading. One observation he makes on Coleridge's theory, however, seems to me mistaken. Whereas Coleridge

---

[19] Orsini, *Coleridge and German Idealism*, p. 169; Krieger, *Theory of Criticism* (Baltimore: The Johns Hopkins University Press, 1967), p. 112n.

[20] *Biographia*, II, 30.

The Universal Principle

always represents the difference between copy and imitation as one of kind, Father Appleyard sees them only as two degrees of artistic representation. Referring to the illustrations from the drama, he notes that even the most realistic play is still not real life but a "product of artistic making."[21] But this observation, though undeniable in itself, misses an essential point of Coleridge's view. If the realistic stage play is patently not real life, neither is the marble peach a real peach. Coleridge's objection to these copyings of reality is neither the success nor the failure of their delusive aim but their aesthetic poverty. The "artist" in such cases, aiming only at facsimile, achieves only the degree of distance from reality imposed by the material conditions of his making: no peach was ever marble and the doings of people in real life are modally discrepant from the fictionality of stage-setting and acting. Knowing this, the copy-maker does his best to avoid a further marring of his fidelity by any "infusion of [his] own knowledge and talent." He wants it to be as lifelike as possible. If, as Father Appleyard would have it, the difference were only one of degree, it would still be so great as to produce a critical disparity of value that makes itself felt in experience. However logically impeccable, no theory can claim our assent that fails to allow for the vast difference between seeing *Hamlet* and seeing a skillful television soap opera, obviously a much more faithful mirroring of real life than Shakespeare's tragedy.

Reference to a specific aesthetic experience is a reminder that no more than any other analyst since his day did Coleridge open the arcanum of artistic creation to the daylight of full understanding. Artistic creation, Carl Jung has assured us, "will for ever elude the human understanding. It can only be described in its manifestations; it can be obscurely

[21] *Coleridge's Philosophy of Literature* (Cambridge: Harvard University Press, 1965), pp. 109-110.

sensed, but never wholly grasped." And so Coleridge's *imitation*, even after its attributes have been identified, remains a mysteriously value-fraught product, a *tertium aliquid*, as he is obliged to call it,[22] generated by the beneficial antagonism of the imagination's polar opposites. Because in itself the product is finally ineffable, he can discuss it only in relation to the two other terms of what we might call the aesthetic triad: nature (reality), the mindless copy, and (*pace* Father Appleyard) the generically separate imitation. However imperfect its logical exposition, Coleridge's intuitive grasp of this problem deserves serious attention if only because so many other writers since his time, especially creative artists, have confirmed it. D. H. Lawrence, considering van Gogh's painted sunflowers, is one of a long list:

His painting does not represent the sunflower itself. . . . And the camera will visualise the sunflower far more perfectly than van Gogh can.

For Lawrence, as for Coleridge, the miraculous creation is a "third something" (*tertium aliquid*), the resultant of nature and human ingenuity.

The vision on the canvas is a third thing, utterly intangible and inexplicable, the offspring of the sunflower itself and van Gogh himself. The vision on the canvas is for ever incommensurable with the canvas, or the paint, or van Gogh as a human organism, or the sunflower as a botanical organism. You cannot weigh nor measure nor even describe the vision on the canvas. It exists, to tell the truth, only in the much-debated fourth-dimension. In dimensional space it has no existence.[23]

---

[22] Jung, *Modern Man in Search of a Soul* (New York: Harcourt, Brace, n.d.), p. 177; *Biographia*, I, 198.

[23] D. H. Lawrence, *Selected Literary Criticism*, ed. Anthony Beal (New York: Viking Press, 1967), p. 108.

IV

Organic Mimesis and Poetic Art

"Imitation," Coleridge explained,

is the mesothesis of likeness and difference. The difference is as essential to it as the likeness; for without the difference, it would be a copy or facsimile. But to borrow a term from astronomy, it is a liberating mesothesis: for it may verge more to likeness as in painting, or more to difference, as in sculpture.

Although this passage from Table Talk is probably his most succinct definition of the "universal principle," the central role it plays in his poetics becomes clear only when he applies it to the other arts. Besides the illustrations already noted (from opera, stage scenery, and landscape painting), there is another from an art which had its heyday in the previous century. In the pleasure we experience at the sight of a fine landscape garden, he sees the type of that mimetic restructuring of reality which we enjoy in a good drama.

"How natural!" we say; but the very wonder that furnished the how implies that we perceived art at the same moment. We catch the hint from nature itself. Whenever in mountains or cataracts we discover a likeness to anything

Organic Mimesis and Poetic Art

artificial, which we yet know was not artificial, what pleasure! So in appearances known to be artificial that appear natural.

So, that is, in works of art, whose appeal depends on their *being perceived as artificial*, a cardinal point in Kant's aesthetics. The relative worthlessness of copyist "art"—transcripts of the language of common men in poems as well as marble peaches in bowls—is precisely its aim to suppress our perception of its artificiality.[1]

One of Coleridge's marginal notes on this issue links drama and the dance. Shakespeare's plays, being imitations, "take from real life all that is what it ought to be, and supply the rest," while modern plays sought merely "to *copy* what is, as it is. . . ." He underscores the stark heterogeneity of these two exemplars of dramatic art by observing that the difference between life and art that is an essential element in Shakespeare appears as an unintentional defect in the inept naturalistic productions of the current playwrights. An illustration from an imagined ballet with which this note ends gives direct expression to the often tacit psychological aspect of Coleridge's aesthetic thought. "We should think it strange," it occurs to him, "if a tale in *dance* were announced, and the actors did not dance at all. Yet such is modern comedy."[2] The mimicry of a copy, that is, constitutes a sort of breach of mimetic promise, a disappoint-

---

[1] *Table Talk* (New York: R. Worthington, 1884), p. 265; *Shakespearean Criticism*, I, 181. Raysor notes the conceptual parallel with Kant here. Schelling thought painting differed from sculpture in that the former "does not present its images as being the objects themselves, but expressly wishes them to be looked on as images." "Concerning the Relation of the Plastic Arts to Nature," in Herbert Read, *The True Voice of Feeling* (New York: Pantheon, 1953), p. 348.

[2] *Miscellaneous Criticism*, p. 49.

ment of a set of expectations aroused in the audience by the very conventions of stage and actors. In exactly parallel fashion (as we shall see below) Coleridge will condemn prosaic phraseology in verse as a violation of the linguistic promise enunciated by the fact of metrical form.

Since the modern plays Coleridge had in mind were, most of them, not verse dramas, he obviously recognized a fact for which his theory made imperfect provision: that even in prose the representation of conversation must be an imitation, not a copy. His opposition of these two terms and his analysis of the conditions which govern their operancy can provide theoretical ground for a phenomenon of mimetic art to which other critics have borne witness. It was Henrik Ibsen's signal contribution to the revitalization of European drama, Georg Lukacs writes, that

when dialogue had lost most of its dramatic tension and had degenerated into a gramophone record of everyday speech, Ibsen wrote . . . a dialogue which was in a much deeper sense true to life than any mere copy of everyday conversation could ever be.[3]

Perhaps the most revealing example of Coleridge's principle occurs in his letter to the comic actor Charles Mathews, which grounds the kinship of the histrionic to the other arts in their common mimetic nature. Acting, too, is an imitation, which

of necessity implies & demands difference—*whereas a Copy aims at* identity. *What a marble peach on a mantlepiece, that you take up deluded, & put down with pettish disgust, is compared with a fruit-piece of Vanhuysen's,*

---

[3] *Studies in European Realism* (New York: Grosset and Dunlap, 1964), p. 133.

Organic Mimesis and Poetic Art

even such is a mere Copy *of nature compared with a true histrionic* Imitation. *A good actor is Pygmalion's Statue, a work of Exquisite art, animated & gifted with motion, but still art, still a species of* Poetry.

Mathews, one may guess, must have been gratified by this exaltation of his profession to the level of a fine art. But however motivated it may have been by a generous impulse to compliment, any doubt that Coleridge meant every syllable of what he wrote is dispelled by a letter to Byron written only a few months later, in 1815, which reports his delight at the performance of an actress named Hudson. This illustration is especially germane to poetics because it concerns her recitation of Shakespearean blank verse. Miss Hudson steered a happy course between an overstress of the iambic beat and the opposite fault, which,

substituting copy *for* Imitation *and assuming that the actor cannot speak too like natural talking, destroys all sense of metre—and consequently, if it be metre, converts the language into a sort of Prose intolerable to a good ear.*

Anyone who has fidgeted through a performance of a Shakespearean tragedy by actors determined at all costs to sound "natural" will appreciate the force of Coleridge's observation.[4]

But how does Coleridge's imitation relate to the

[4] *Letters*, III, 501; IV, 599. Coleridge's *imitation* occupies the happy medium between the pointless conflation of art and life and a denaturalized formalism. The opposing failures of Shakespearean recitation perfectly illustrate its vital importance. "A good actor," W. H. Auden writes, "must—alas, today he too seldom does—make the audience hear Shakespeare's lines as verse not prose, but if he tries to make the verse sound like a different language, he will make himself ridiculous." *The Dyer's Hand* (New York: Random House, 1962), pp. 24-25.

other cardinal principles of his literary and aesthetic theory, since these too affect his conception of poetic language? It may be well to state initially that, as other analysts have pointed out, Coleridge's thought is highly eclectic, blending ideas of divergent intellectual ancestry. Although I think it might be shown that this is less true of his literary criticism than it is of his philosophical, theological, and political thinking, this acknowledgment is made to prevent any inference that the following remarks assume, or are meant to show, that even here his reasoning has the systematic seamlessness of a Kant's or a Collingwood's. Its virtue lies not so much in its internal consistency as in the imaginative brilliance by which ideas of varied philosophic origin are made to collaborate in the elucidation of an issue lying at the heart of literary theory.

Some of Coleridge's celebrated doctrines and definitions that elude ready articulation with his mimetic theory may at least be shown not to clash with it. J. A. Appleyard and W. J. Bate have both suggested its close kinship to the definition of *symbol* in *The Statesman's Manual*, which is always an actual part of what it stands for. That poetic language is in this sense symbolic as well as an imitation seems implicit in Coleridge's description of Shakespeare's language. Since he locates this in a mean between, or blend of, human speech and the "language" of nature, such that it becomes "a part of that which it manifests," one readily shares Gerald Bruns' recognition of at least a formulaic link here between symbol and poetic utterance.[5]

---

[5] Appleyard, *Coleridge's Philosophy of Literature* (Cambridge: Harvard University Press, 1965), pp. 107; Bate, *Coleridge* (New York: Macmillan, 1968), p. 164; *Shakespearean Criticism*, I, 185; Bruns, *Modern Poetry and the Idea of Language* (New Haven: Yale University Press, 1974), p. 53.

Organic Mimesis and Poetic Art

More than one modern critic has fixed on semantic reflexivity as the characteristic feature of the poetic symbol. Philip Wheelwright may have been unconsciously following Coleridge when he described poetic language ("the plurisign, the poetic symbol") as part of its own designation.[6] But since, to my knowledge, Coleridge nowhere directly equates *symbol* and *imitation*, we are not justified in supposing he considered the two terms interchangeable. Moreover, as regards the language of poetry, we should note further that the phrase "the language of Shakespeare" may refer to prose as well as verse.

Surely it is easy to see how the pretense to literal fidelity that characterizes the copy must inhibit that momentary willing suspension of disbelief—to invoke Coleridge's most parroted formula—on which artistic illusion (not delusion) depends. Among Wordsworth's poetic defects he condemns a matter-of-factness produced by the laborious minuteness of representation necessary to win assent to statements in real life but offensive in poetry, where the reader "is willing to believe for his own sake." The negative faith of poetic illusion, which enables us willingly to suspend judgment as to the real existence of poetic images is estopped by the intrusion of "words and facts of known and absolute truth." Elsewhere, speaking of Shakespeare's *Tempest*, he sets forth the interdependence of genuine imitation and the qualities of "poetic probability" and dramatic illusion which are destroyed by the literalism of a mere copy.[7]

For the student of his theory of poetic language, however, the most crucial conceptual link joins imitation to organic unity and the function of the creative

---

[6] "On the Semantics of Poetry," in *Essays on the Language of Literature*, ed. Seymour Chatman and Samuel R. Levin (Boston: Houghton-Mifflin, 1967), p. 254.

[7] *Biographia*, II, 101, 107; *Shakespearean Criticism*, II, 258.

imagination. A comparison of his several references to imitation makes it clear that the vital "mesothesis of likeness and difference" which structures an imitation is an instance of the opposites which the poet's imagination reconciles in dynamic tension. "All Imitation in the Fine Arts," as in one place he specifically declares, "is the union of Disparate Things." The relation of mimesis to the doctrine of reconciled opposites takes its most cogent form in the eighteenth chapter of the *Biographia*, and precisely in refutation of Wordsworth's claim that no essential stylistic difference exists between verse and prose. Meter, Coleridge reasons, far from being the mere pleasant but unessential superaddition of Wordsworth's supposing, is "the proper form of poetry," lacking which it is simply defective. As Wordsworth himself had admitted, poetry implies passion, Coleridge supplying the refinement that the very act of poetic composition generates this passion, which in turn demands (and in fact produces) a language correspondingly different from that of prose. He then adds that a closely related principle, "if not the same argument in a more general form," states that every part of an organized whole must be adjusted to the more important parts. Finally, he declares this whole chain of reasoning to be strengthened by the reflection that poetry is an imitative art; and—in yet another version of his basic idea—

imitation, as opposed to copying, consists either in the interfusion of the SAME throughout the radically DIFFERENT, or of the different throughout a base radically the same. [8]

If poetry is quintessentially an imitative art, and if imitation enforces a reconciliation of opposites, then

[8] *Notebooks*, III, entry 4397; *Biographia*, II, 55-56.

Organic Mimesis and Poetic Art

Coleridge's identification of metrical form as the ideal condition of versified expression becomes impeccably logical when set in the context of his understanding of meter itself. This he ascribes to what he nicely labels a "salutary antagonism" between the emotion contemplated by the poet in the excitement of creation and a spontaneous effort to hold it in check. Whatever else it may be then, meter is a mechanism of control, a technique of mimetic mastery available to the creative imagination, which, we recall, reconciles among other discordant elements "a more than usual state of emotion, with a more than usual order,"[9] in this case the order imposed by the isometric segmentation of the verse line.

In what is at best a grudging estimate of Coleridge as critic, F. R. Leavis once conceded that he did perceive certain essential truths about poetic rhythm and meter that had still not become staples of academic literary study at that time. In the view of one skilled modern metrist, however, his "demonstration" of the organic character of meter has predominated in poetics ever since. As Coleridge sees it, meter is not a strand of a poetic texture irrelevant to and dislocative of a logical structure, as at one stage of his career John Crowe Ransom would have it. It is if anything indispensably relevant to a verbal ordonnance to which the logical syntax of prose imperfectly con-

[9] *Biographia*, II, 49, 12. Another Coleridgean discovery since become a theoretical commonplace. This is no proper occasion for tracing its metamorphic progress through modern poetics, but a sample may be enlightening for its faintly patronizing tone. In a chapter of *The Poetic Mind* (New York: Macmillan, 1922), significantly entitled "The Impulse and the Control," F. C. Prescott founds verse rhythm and meter in a conflict between passionate impulse and its control. "Coleridge is on the right track when he finds the origin of metre in 'the balance in the mind effected by that spontaneous effort which strives to hold in check the workings of passion' " (p. 241).

forms. If Coleridge's accounting seems at last the more convincing, its superiority is in part traceable to the more sophisticated psychology of composition on which it rests. The interaction between conscious intention and spontaneous impulse of Coleridge's etiology (described below) contrasts starkly with Ransom's reduction of the labor of composition to "a verbal exercise in search of a language which on the one hand would 'make the meter' and on the other hand would 'make the sense.' "[10]

For his ascription of the elements of meter to a spontaneous impulse caused by an unusual degree of excitement Coleridge can offer no exhaustive explanation. For its validation we do best to rely on the testimony of other poets, on Pope's boasting (after Ovid) in *An Epistle to Dr. Arbuthnot* of a precocity that "lisped in numbers." Or, if Pope's report, being itself poetry, is suspect, we have the sober prose of T. S. Eliot, who confesses his own inability to explain.

The human soul, in intense emotion, strives to express itself in verse. It is not for me, but for the neurologists, to discover why this is so, and why and how feeling and rhythm are related. [11]

Whatever its limitations, Coleridge's grasp of the origin and effects of meter is central to his understanding of the poetic function of language. To come at this understanding he adopted the traditional strategy of discriminating the styles of verse and prose, a procedure which he considered indispensable to a satisfactory resolution of the whole *quaestio*

---

[10] Leavis, "Coleridge," in *The Importance of Scrutiny*, ed. Eric Bentley (New York: George Stewart, 1948), p. 82; Ransom, *The New Criticism* (Norfolk, Conn.: New Directions, 1941), p. 294.

[11] *Biographia*, II, 50; Eliot, *Selected Essays* (New York: Harcourt, Brace, 1950), p. 34.

vexata. In this respect his approach resembles most others, the difference lying in the greater precision, complication, and penetration of Coleridge's version. By his day, to name meter as the differentia, *tout court*, of poetic style was as stale as it was sterile. His theory represents a great advance because in earlier poetics meter appears either as one of several distinguishing marks of verse, on a par with its various syntactic peculiarities, or else as *the* feature accounting for both poetry's variation from and superiority to prose. In radical contrast to these conventional views, meter for Coleridge, though nothing or almost nothing in isolation, is nonetheless the form in which the peculiarities (inversion, figurative language, the aural devices of rhyme, assonance, etc.) attain their fullest effect. It is, as it were, the sensuous correlative of the verbal *ordonnance* (Coleridge's word for it in the *Biographia*) of poetic expression, and its justification. Meter thus functions in verse in a manner rather like that of a catalyst in a chemical reaction; or, in Coleridge's own more accurate image, it is like yeast, valueless or even disagreeable in itself but enlivening the liquor in which it is contained. Considered in isolation, he affirms in the passage most directly contradicting his friend's equation of prose and verse, meter.

is simply a stimulant of the attention, and therefore excites the question: Why is the attention to be thus stimulated? Now the question cannot be answered by the pleasure of the metre itself: for this we have shown to be conditional, *and dependent on the appropriateness of the thoughts and expressions, to which the metrical form is superadded. Neither can I conceive any other answer that can be rationally given, short of this: I write in metre, because I am about to use a language different from that of prose.* [12]

[12] *Biographia*, II, 52, 53.

The difference in question has of course nothing to do with a special vocabulary. It is stylistic, not lexical: "Poetry justifies, as *Poetry* independent of every other Passion, some new combination of Language, & *commands* the omission of many others allowable in other compositions." This sentence, from an 1802 letter to William Sotheby,[13] sums up Coleridge's theory in its three interdependent heads. First, verse is a mode of expression characterized by a unique verbal ordonnance. Second, the passion that generates both that ordonnance and its accompanying metrical form is primarily the passion of the mimetic activity itself, not any emotional quality resident in the subject or occasion of the poem. Meter is thus the sensible manifestation of the polar tension that marks off imitation from copy. Third is the express denial that metrical form can "naturalize" an inherently prosaic vocabulary.

This last principle has special interest as a point of contrast between Coleridge's poetics and certain current views it otherwise resembles and supports. There is, for example, an obvious consonance between Coleridge's prosody and Roman Jakobson's doctrine that "poeticalness is not a supplementation of discourse with rhetorical ornament but a total re-evaluation of the discourse and of all its components whatever." Quite clearly it was Coleridge's ready perception of this linguistic phenomenon that prompted his dissent from Wordsworth's notion of verse as the mere superaddition of meter to an order of discourse essentially prosaic. But Jakobson goes further. His suggestive maxim that the poetic function projects the principle of equivalence from the axis of selection to that of combination entails a qualitative change in poetic language far more exclusive,

[13] *Letters*, II, 812.

absolute, and, as it were, automatic than that envisaged by Coleridge. "So in poetry," Jakobson concludes, "any verbal element is converted into a figure of poetic speech." In the *Biographia* probably the best known of several sentences nearly corresponding to this principle runs: "If metre be superadded, all other parts must be made consonant with it." The clear implication, as against Jakobson, is that the necessary conversion is not inevitable, a fact borne out by the painful occurrence of prosaic lines in otherwise excellent poems.[14]

This reservation is not intended in disparagement of Jakobson's poetics as against Coleridge's, nor does it logically enforce any such appraisal. In fact, the divergence between Coleridge and Jakobson may be more verbal than substantive. Certainly they seem very nearly to coincide when Jakobson denies that meter alone can make a poem. Meter is an instance of his "poetic function," but for metrical discourse to become poetry that function must be *dominant*. It is not so, he says, in the mnemonic jingle "Thirty Days Hath September." This homely example reveals the virtual identity of conception on this point between Jakobson's structuralist theory and Coleridge's analysis in the *Biographia*, Chapter XIV. Only in the lowest sense of the term, Coleridge argues, might anyone call "Thirty Days Hath September" and other metrical pieces "of the same class and purpose" poems. They are not truly so, however, since they aim at "a different object." In Jakobson's system, Coleridge's *object* is more sharply discriminated in the term *function*, used in the linguistic sense derived from K. Buhler's *Sprachtheorie*.[15]

[14] "Linguistics and Poetics," in *Essays on the Language of Literature*, p. 321; *Biographia*, II, 9-10.
[15] "Linguistics and Poetics," p. 304; *Biographia*, II, 8-9.

In any case, at the moment I am concerned only with placing in relief the main tenets of Coleridge's description of poetic discourse. One such, already touched on, is a corollary of the mutual adjustment of meter and poetic language: that a certain phraseology, certain patterns of expression, admissible in prose, are positively incompatible with the rhythmical regularity of meter. Wordsworth's neglect of this rule, whether from his mistaken theory or (what seems more likely) from momentary lapses of taste, produced that occasional bathos that Coleridge deplores as a blemish in some of his best poems.

In all written discourse Coleridge discerns three species of style: one peculiar to verse, one proper only to prose, and a neutral third common to both. The admissible presence of the last in almost all poems except the shortest is what prompts his observation that "a poem of any length neither can be, or ought to be, all poetry." Why this is so is perhaps less clearly explained in the *Biographia* than in T. S. Eliot's independent formulation of the same insight:

in a poem of any length, there must be transitions between passages of greater and less intensity, to give a rhythm of fluctuating emotion essential to the musical structure of the whole; and the passages of less intensity will be prosaic—so that . . . it may be said that no poet can write a poem of magnitude unless he is a master of the prosaic.[16]

(Coleridge himself, be it noted, was confident that any true poet was *eo ipso* a good prose writer.) Some admirable poems—he offers in evidence narrative passages from Chaucer's *Troilus* and George Her-

---

[16] *Biographia*, II, 97, 11; Eliot, *On Poetry and Poets* (New York: Farrar, Straus, and Cudahy, 1957), pp. 24-25.

Organic Mimesis and Poetic Art

bert's verses—he adjudges to be entirely in the neutral style. Samuel Daniel's *Hymen's Triumph*, another such, contrasts favorably in this respect with his *Civil Wars*, marred as it is by a "frequent incorrespondency of his diction to his metre."[17]

Coleridge's rejection of Wordsworth's argument in the Preface to *Lyrical Ballads* therefore reduces itself to the contention that there are "modes of expression" natural to prose but foreign to verse and, vice versa, an alternate mode in the language of verse that would be vicious in good prose. The very strength of his conviction on this point makes it regrettable that Coleridge cites no example of this viciously poetic prose to balance his several citations of prosaic verse. But most readers can no doubt think of cases of the kind of meretricious rhetoric he has in mind. As it is, he alludes only to a related fault, of which Charles Dickens provides examples often noticed with disapproval today: prose writers "constantly slipping into scraps of metre."[18]

Although Wordsworth is not without his modern defenders, the most advanced twentieth-century poetics confirms Coleridge's generic dichotomy of verse and prose styles. Like Jakobson, and sometimes under his influence, almost every structuralist who has investigated poetic language reaches a similar conclusion. We read of "the special kind of language which is poetry," of "une syntaxe proprement poétique," designed not for the communicative function of prose but for "quelque chose de radicalement autre." Generally speaking, recent analysis has been less successful at defining (or even recognizing) Coleridge's neutral style. Yet the inadequacy of a simple dichotomy to deal with the stylistic gradations of verse is appar-

[17] *Miscellaneous Criticism*, pp. 219-220; *Biographia*, II, 71-73, 61.
[18] *Biographia*, II, 49; *Miscellaneous Criticism*, p. 220.

ent in much recent discussion. Jorge Guillen, who like the rest holds that poetry is simply written "in a certain key," offers no explanation of why (as indeed he does notice) some prosaic turns of phrase lose their prosaic quality when used in verse. And surely Coleridge's triple distinction might have helped Jean Cohen avoid the terminologically contradictory result of his tortuous analysis: that a poetic utterance is at the same time verse and prose ("Le message poétique est à la fois vers et prose").[19]

It should be stressed that for all his exaltation of his own art Coleridge was far from indifferent to what Dryden called "the other harmony." In fact he studied the art and progress of English prose from the Renaissance to his own day, giving detailed reasons for his preference of pre-Restoration prose to that of the eighteenth century. Prose was the lesser art but an art nonetheless, to be savored by readers and appraised by critics. His relative valuation is perhaps best conveyed by his somewhat parochial analogy: prose is a gentleman, poetry a Christian clergyman, i.e. "the *Apotheosis* of a Gentleman." In any case, the honorable status accorded the art of a nonmetrical composition in Coleridge's criticism is signaled by his being always careful to posit not a dual but a tripartite division of human utterance: verse, prose, and conversation. Accordingly, not only verse but prose too,

---

[19] The quoted phrases are from Archibald A. Hill, "Poetry and Stylistics," in *Essays on the Language of Literature*, p. 387; Mikel Dufrenne, *Le Poétique*, 2nd ed. (Paris: Presses Universitaires de France, 1973), p. 102; and Jean Cohen, *Structure du langage poétique* (Paris: Flammarion, 1966), p. 96. Cohen's extreme position defines poetry as anti-prose. Guillen, *Language and Poetry* (Cambridge: Harvard University Press, 1961), p. 215; Cohen, *Structure du langage poétique*, p. 101.

at least in all argumentative and consecutive works, differs, and ought to differ, from the language of conversation; even as reading ought to differ from talking.[20]

And here is another of those salutary but long unnoticed *aperçus* in Coleridge's poetics that have had to await twentieth-century resuscitation—with, as usual, no acknowledgment of his precedence. Somewhat amusingly, it is rather a fictional personnage, Molière's M. Jourdain, who is credited with the discovery. T. S. Eliot leads the parade of modern proponents of the "Jourdain doctrine":

But M. Jourdain was right . . . he did not speak prose—he only talked. For I mean to draw a triple distinction: between prose, and verse, and our ordinary speech which is mostly below the level of either verse or prose.

Next comes Northrop Frye, to tell a university audience that "M. Jourdain had not been speaking prose all his life, and prose is not the language of ordinary speech." John Hollander has also argued that much "modernist" poetics—he instances Charles Olson's "Projective Verse"—is bedeviled by critics who have followed M. Jourdain's tutor in their failure to separate speech from prose. Nor are the amiable bourgeois' defenders confined to writers in English. The Argentinian Juan Luis Borges also chides M. Jour-

[20] *Letters*, VI, 928; *Biographia*, II, 45-46. When it first appeared, Coleridge thought, "prose must have struck men with greater *admiration* than poetry. In the latter it was the language of passion and emotion; it is what they themselves spoke and heard in moments of exultation, indignation, etc. But to have an evolving roll, or a succession of leaves, talk continuously the language of deliberate reason in a form of continued preconception, of a Z already possessed when A is being uttered,—this must have appeared *god*-like." *Miscellaneous Criticism*, p. 227.

dain's mentor for "correcting" his pupil's naive wisdom in the matter. "One doesn't speak in prose, one tries to make oneself understood." To put one's thoughts to paper, Borges says, is to attempt prose and therefore to face "a different set of problems." The most recent vindicator of M. Jourdain I have come upon is the Spanish critic Fernando Lázaro Carreter, who puts the issue in terms of what he calls "literal" language, meaning utterance designed to endure, to be read beyond the purposes of nonce communication. Though his formulation derives explicitly from modern linguistic concepts, it is perhaps as close to Coleridge's line of reasoning as any other. "The opposition prose/verse," Carreter writes,

can only be established in the heart of literal language. The only way of producing nonliteral language is conversation. When the philosophy professor revealed to M. Jourdain that he spoke in prose, the professor taught him something totally incorrect. [21]

Directly or by obvious implication these modern writers confirm the point of Coleridge's three-way division which is most important for defining poetic language. They all range the artificial forms of verse and prose against the natural form of oral speech. The theoretical consequences are several. To mention—for the moment—only one, the radical realism of Wordsworth's derivation of poetic language from rustic speech must directly contradict his stylistic

[21] Eliot, *On Poetry and Poets*, p. 76; Frye, *The Well-Tempered Critic* (Bloomington: Indiana University Press, 1963), p. 18; Hollander, *Vision and Resonance* (New York: Oxford, 1975), p. 239; Borges, *Borges on Writing*, ed. Norman di Giovanni, Daniel Halpern, and Frank MacShane (New York: Dutton, 1973), p. 76; Carreter, "The Literal Message," *Critical Inquiry*, III (1976), 326. It is worth noting that traditional stylistics had separated prose from conversation, as for example in Buffon's *Discours sur le style*.

Organic Mimesis and Poetic Art

equation of verse and prose. Curiously, modern linguistic poetics has yet to purge itself of this counsel-darkening conflation of modes. "Le langage naturel, par définition," writes Jean Cohen, "c'est la prose. La poésie est langage d'art, c'est-à-dire artifice."[22]

Two aspects of Coleridge's theory want clarification. One relates to the separate definitions of *poetry* and *poem* given in Chapter XIV of *Biographia Literaria*. In a vain attempt to follow Coleridge's reasoning Allen Tate once damned the passage in question as "probably the most confused statement ever uttered by a great critic." Though he holds that verse is the perfect form of poetic expression and that meter in prose is repulsive, Coleridge nonetheless recognizes the existence of poetry in prose form, even "poetry of the highest kind." From this it might appear that he was not much luckier than his critical predecessors at clarifying this old dilemma. If metrical form is the perfection of poetic expression, how can the non-metrical Book of Isaiah be, as he declares it to be in many of its parts, "poetry in the most emphatic sense"? So superlative a characterization surely precludes the inference that its poetical quality would be enhanced if it were written in meter. If we turn for enlightenment to his definitions of *poetry* and *poem*, we learn only that Isaiah, being poetry, must reconcile opposing elements; and that *not* being a poem, its component parts (if any) do not produce a gratification distinct from that of the whole (if any).[23] But how is this reconcilement of opposites manifested? It is hard to imagine any means other than those very stylistic features which mark off the poetic from the

---

[22] "Natural language is by definition prose. Poetry is the language of art, that is, a contrivance." *Structure du langage poétique*, p. 48.

[23] Tate, "Literature as Knowledge," in *Essays of Four Decades* (Chicago: The Swallow Press, 1968), p. 94; *Biographia*, II, 11, 10.

prose style. Yet it is precisely these features that both require the rhythmical pulsations of meter for their consummation and justify its operancy. And so we come full circle.

Moreover, the dilemma seems only deepened by the reflection that, for all Coleridge tells us to the contrary, a given piece of poetic prose may contain proportionately more poetry than a given poem (unless very short). Any reader may be forgiven for thinking that Coleridge judged poetic prose to be, potentially at least, a richer form of expression than that found in poems properly so called. Since in the context of his own poetic convictions this would be patently absurd, the only possible conclusion is that Coleridge's terms *poetry* and *poem*, *poetic* and *poematic*, designate not two degrees of expressive power but two distinct kinds of utterance, of which the poematic is the more intense. Such a generic division of styles is signaled by the reference to poetic and poematic diction in the letter to Edward Coleridge cited above (II, 34). Unfortunately, it is more often obscured by Coleridge's alternate use of the word *poetry* to designate both a general artistic quality and compositions in verse exclusively. This ambiguity haunts his assertion, for example, that meter is the proper form of poetry. To be faithful to his desynonymization, and to his obvious meaning, he ought to have said that meter was the form proper to the poematic ordonnance. Allen Tate's judgment that Coleridge's definition of poetry has probably been more harmful to critical thought than anything any other critic has ever said is surely excessive.[24] On the other hand, its author's own stylistic imprecision is almost certainly the major reason why it has not been, as it becomes when rightly understood, a most salutary contribution to modern poetics.

[24] "Literature as Knowledge," p. 94.

The fact is, though, that Coleridge becomes progressively more careful not to obscure the difference between the two forms of artistic use of language. In 1803 he apparently felt no need for further discrimination in proposing to Southey a history of poetry, including "all prose truly poetical." In 1811 he informed a lecture audience that poetry was the language of heaven, its "exquisite delight" giving a foretaste of the celestial joy. All doubt that he reserved such rhapsodic praise for metrical poetry alone is finally removed by a marginal note of 1823 to Milton's *Comus* in Thomas Warton's edition of the *Poems on Several Occasions*, which invites us to compare a beautiful passage describing the Indian fig tree, in Book IX of *Paradise Lost*, with its prose source in Gerard's *Herball*; or Shakespeare's description of Cleopatra in her barge with the prose version of that scene in North's *Plutarch*. Either comparison, he wrote, would convincingly demonstrate

the charm and effect *of metre and the* art *of poetry, independent of the thoughts and images—the superiority, in short, of* poematic *over* prose *composition, the poetry or no-poetry being the same in both.* . . . [25]

A second point in need of clarification in Coleridge's poetics has to do with the relation of passion and meter. In *Biographia,* Chapter XVIII, he begins his analysis by tracing the origin of meter to an antagonism between passion and a spontaneous mental effort to check it. This spontaneous effort is also, at first, as natural as the passion which occasions it. But in a second stage of the creative process (because this is what Coleridge is describing), the poet's conscious will supervenes to organize these impulses into meter

[25] *Letters*, II, 955; *Shakespearean Criticism*, II, 34; *Miscellaneous Criticism*, p. 181.

in the formal sense. From these data, no doubt derived mainly from introspection of his own creative experience, he deduces the two "legitimate conditions" required of metrical composition:

First, that, as the elements *of metre owe their existence to a state of increased excitement, so the metre itself should be accompanied by the natural language of excitement. Secondly, that as these elements are formed into metre* artificially, *by a* voluntary *act, with the design and for the purpose of blending* delight *with emotion, so the traces of present* volition *should throughout the metrical language be proportionately discernible. Now these two conditions must be reconciled and co-present. There must be not only a partnership, but a union; an interpenetration of passion and of will, of* spontaneous *impulse and of* voluntary *purpose.* [26]

This remarkable explication is further evidence of how consistently Coleridge's metrical theory accords with his governing doctrine of the imagination as a reconciler of opposites. But to grasp its full import it must also be read with a steady awareness of its relation to his equally determinant concept of a genuine imitation, here invoked by the requirement that "the

---

[26] *Biographia*, II, 49-50. "N.b. how by excitement of the Associative Power Passion itself imitates Order, and the *order* resulting produces a pleasurable *Passion* (whence Metre) and elevates the Mind by making its feelings the Objects of its reflection and how recalling the Sights and Sounds that had accompanied the occasions of the original passion it impregnates them with an interest not their own by means of the Passions, and yet tempers the passion by the calming power which all *distinct* images exert on the human soul." *Notebooks*, III, entry 4397. Miss Coburn's note on this entry calls attention to its "Schillerian undertones." But the general influence of Schiller on Coleridge's aesthetics does not preclude an even greater role played by his own creative experience in his understanding of how the poet shapes his emotions into art.

Organic Mimesis and Poetic Art

traces of present *volition* should throughout . . . be proportionately discernible." It was, we recall, a condition raising it above a mere copy that the pleasure afforded by an imitation depends on its being *perceived* to be the result of purposeful art.

But the phrase most pertinent to our chief concern states that meter "should be accompanied by the natural language of excitement." Where this is not the case, the poet has in effect violated the tacit compact between himself and his reader implied by his use of meter in the first place. Of this violation Coleridge found Wordsworth too often guilty. In such narrative pieces as "Simon Lee," "Alice Fell," and parts of "The Sailor's Mother" he was unable to discover any justification for their being in metrical form.[27]

As Coleridge sees it, poetic language no less than meter originates in passion. They are the offspring of a common psychic impulse. The distinctive features of poetic syntax, unless they are prompted by mental excitement, are only tasteless verbal posturings. Inversions, for example, result from the train of thought being directed by passion. Forgetting this, Walter Scott had marred his *Lady of the Lake* by inverting in order to accommodate his meter and rhyme, or simply to disguise colloquial phraseology. Shakespeare, Coleridge predictably observes, never

[27] *Biographia*, II, 50, 53-54. Wordsworth had alluded to such a compact in the Preface. Coleridge's account of a linguistic stance which the reader of a poem is "entitled to expect" constitutes another of his anticipations of structuralist doctrine. See, *e.g.*, Jonathan Culler's idea of genres as signaling "sets of expectations" in the reader. *Structuralist Poetics* (Ithaca: Cornell University Press, 1975), p. 129. But this general notion as an element of aesthetic experience is hardly a structuralist "discovery." In 1941 J. C. Ransom observed that above "every poem which looks like a poem is a sign which reads: This road does not go through to action; fictitious." *The World's Body* (Port Washington, N. Y.: Kennikat Press, 1964), p. 131.

does so. Justified always by some logic of thought, if not of passion, his syntactical transpositions are never imposed for metrical convenience. Similarly in *Paradise Lost*, where, more than in any other poem, language and verse structure mutually correspond. An order of words and sentences felt to be unnatural by both Samuel Johnson and T. S. Eliot, Coleridge praises as "exquisitely artificial: but the position [of the words] is rather according to the logic of passion or universal logic, than to the logic of grammar." Meter too, although ordered by the poet's conscious art, properly arises only "where the feeling calls for it." Coleridge also easily intuited what Edward Sapir has since affirmed: that "the poet's rhythms can only be a more sensitive and stylicized application of rhythmic tendencies that are characteristic of the daily speech of his people." In this regard Coleridge thought English poets were especially favored. "Our language," he wrote,

gives to expression a certain measure, and will, in a strong state of passion, admit of scansion from the very mouth.

To honor his side of the compact, the reader must bring to his aesthetic transaction with the poem a proper state of expectancy.

The very assumption that we are reading the work of a poet supposes that he is in a continuous state of excitement; and thereby arises a language in prose unnatural but in poetry natural. [28]

Few problems of literary theory are more elusive than those encountered in defining prose and verse.

---

[28] *Notebooks*, III, entry 3970; *Shakespearean Criticism*, I, 15; *Miscellaneous Criticism*, pp. 163-164; Sapir, *Language* (New York: Harcourt, Brace, and World, 1949), p. 161; *Shakespearean Criticism*, II, 42.

Organic Mimesis and Poetic Art

Our own century has made little progress toward an agreed-on solution. I. A. Richards, recognizing a "lyrical, or poly-phonic prose," cultivated especially in the last century by essayists like Landor, De Quincey, and Ruskin, posits a stylistic gradation rather than a radical break. Not so Robert Graves, however, who expects "verse to be verse, and prose to be prose." Graves' separatism is confirmed by Valéry as well as by Sir Herbert Read. "There are no degrees of poetry," Read writes. Prose and poetry are simply "distinct in kind."[29]

Generally speaking, Read's conclusion is shared by linguistically oriented analysts of poetic discourse, some of whom have tried to describe it, with various and sometimes suggestive formulations, in syntactic terms. The best known of these is Jakobson's distinction in terms of the selective and combinatory axes of equivalence. For Samuel Levin, the highly effective fusion of form and meaning in poetry, long admired in traditional criticism, is achieved only in a purely linguistic phenomenon which he labels *coupling*, in which semantically and phonetically related syntactic forms coincide. Mikel Dufrenne discovers in prose a predominance of the syntactic over the lexical and in verse the opposite relation. Yet even the most assured and rigorous linguistic stylisticians admit, as Levin concludes early in his treatise, the virtual impossibility of drawing any sharp boundary between poetry and prose. Literary prose, Jean Cohen notes, can differ from verse only in degree ("d'un point de vue quantitatif"). This blurred stylistic boundary is often invoked to argue the futility of all attempts—Coleridge's included—to isolate or even effectively

[29] Richards, *Principles of Literary Criticism* (New York: Harcourt, Brace, n.d.), p. 135; Graves, "Harp, Anvil, Oar," in *The Structure of Verse*, ed. Harvey Gross (Greenwich, Conn.: Fawcett Publications, 1966), p. 66; Read, *The Nature of Literature* (New York: Grove Press, n.d.), p. 68.

describe poetic style. Yet the common experience of readers argues that the difference is there and that it is vital. As to those works hard to locate on either side of the prose-poetry dichotomy, Coleridge himself would have been in hearty accord with Edward Stankiewicz's observation that they have no methodological significance.[30]

It is therefore not surprising to find that not even the intellectual rigor of Coleridge's dissection can avoid some blurring of the generic line between the two styles of written discourse. In one place he presumably admits of *degrees* of passion, so that where it is too weak for formal meter it will at least result in a "language more measured" than usual. Certain affecting passages in the English Bible, he told a lecture audience in 1811, follow, if admittedly not the pure iambics of a Pope, a rhythmic undulation occasionally scannable as classical hexameter:

$$\overline{God}\ \overline{went}|\ \overline{up}\ \overline{with}\ \breve{a}\ |\ \overline{shout},\ \overline{our}$$
$$\overline{Lord}\ \overline{with}\ \overline{the}|\ \overline{sound}\ \breve{of}\ \overline{the}|\ \overline{trumpet}-$$

"so true it is," he concluded, "that wherever passion was, the language became a sort of metre." And this reflection, according to the Tomalin report of this lecture, immediately prompted him to add that verse is not a copy but an imitation of nature.[31]

The evidence seems to indicate that this aesthetically fruitful emotion was aroused not by real experience but by the excitement of poetic composition. A

---

[30] Levin, *Linguistic Structures in Poetry* (The Hague: Mouton, 1962), pp. 37-38, 30; Dufrenne, *Le Poétique*, p. 101; Cohen, *Structure du langage poétique*, p. 149; Stankiewicz, "Linguistics and the Study of Poetic Language," in *Style in Language*, ed. Thomas A. Sebeok (Cambridge: MIT Press, 1960), p. 77.

[31] *Shakespearean Criticism*, II, 52-53.

poem, Coleridge explained, shares with vivid prose writing an expression of human and natural emotions. But for it to become a poem something additional must go into its making: "that pleasurable emotion, that peculiar state and degree of excitement, which arises in the poet himself in the act of composition. . . ." Though curiously neglected in most modern discussions of the nature of poetry, Coleridge's insight confirms an item in the psychology of creativity traditional in Western literary thought. It is the "fervor of poesy," Boccaccio wrote in the fourteenth century, that "impels the soul to a longing for utterance."[32] And Edmund Spenser opened his *Hymn of Heavenly Beauty*

Rapt in the rage of mine own ravisht thought.

But there is also evidence that Coleridge thought the creative act itself to be initiated by some affectively recollected or contemplated idea or experience. Moreover, like many other writers of his time he subscribed to a category of inherently poetic subjects, although he avoided the dogmatic excess of Edgar Poe's flat assertion that a mountain is a more poetic subject than a pair of stairs. To judge from his occasional references to "poetic ideas," his position was closer to Emerson's belief in meter-making arguments or Milton's "thoughts that voluntary move harmonious numbers." He can commend the thoughts in one of Fulke Greville's sonnets for their poetical quality. Exactly the reverse condition, he decided early in life, had marred the style of Pope, in which "matter and diction" struck him as resulting

---

[32] *Ibid.*, I, 147; *Boccaccio on Poetry*, trans. from *Genealogia Deorum Gentilium* by Charles G. Osgood (New York: Bobbs-Merrill, 1956), p. 39.

less from poetic thoughts than from "thoughts *translated* into the language of poetry."[33]

Many earlier critics had paid tribute to the efficacy of meter alone to infuse extraordinary power into ordinary expression. In the Preface to *Lyrical Ballads* Wordsworth himself conceded that Pope had rendered common sense "interesting" by conveying it in verse. But Coleridge, as always, discriminates and, as usual, does so in linguistic or stylistic terms. His concession that a poem of any length cannot be all poetry merely recognizes that meter can naturalize to a poematic environment, so to speak, the neutral style shared by prose and verse. But, in a crucial modification of the view hitherto widely held, he also insisted that meter was powerless to effect this happy transformation where the phraseology was exclusively prosaic.

This last provision of Coleridge's metrical theory can hardly be overstressed. So apparent to thoughtful readers is the link between the beauty of poetic lines and their metrical pattern that some investigators have actually devised experiments to determine how far the aesthetic quality inhered in meter alone. In the eighteenth century Joseph Warton rewrote the fourteen opening lines of Pope's first *Moral Essay* as prose, and then inferred (with a logic now hard to endorse) that the depressing result proved Pope's epistle to be only measured prose. The "scientific" validity of Warton's demonstration is dubious at best, since he not only introduced some slight (but arguably crucial) verbal changes but even suppressed

---

[33] *Miscellaneous Criticism*, p. 243; *Biographia*, I, 11. Coleridge's objection to piscatory eclogues on the grounds that "our feelings have nothing *fishy* in them" perhaps tells us less about his poetics than about his sensibility—or that of Romanticism. See *Miscellaneous Criticism*, p. 244.

Pope's inversions. Recently Jean Cohen performed the same experiment from the opposite direction, putting into enjambed free verse a newspaper report of an auto crash:

Hier, sur la Nationale sept
Une automobile
Roulant à cent à l'heure s'est jetée
Sur un platane
Ses quatre occupants ont été
Tués.

What results, Cohen judges, is not poetry, because it lacks the support of the other devices of verse syntax ("le secours des autres figures"). Yet, he insists, it has become something more than prose, a metamorphosis Cohen can only express by some figurative language of his own. The words, he says, are electrified, as though the drab informational sentence were on the verge "of awaking from its prosaic sleep" simply by virtue of its deviant segmentation ("son découpage aberrant").[34]

Such tests seem entirely justified by the very nature of the theoretical question, even if one is doubtful whether they finally prove too little or too much. In any case, few if any of them consider the negative effect which Coleridge's account provides for: that in some instances meter not only fails to give pleasure but is positively unpleasant. In addition to the instances of this failure culled from Wordsworth, he dared, if only in a marginal jotting, to bring a similar indictment against the ten lines from Milton's *Comus* beginning

---

[34] See the letter to Edward Young prefatory to Warton's *Essay on the Genius and Writings of Pope* (London, 1756, 1782); Cohen, *Structure du langage poétique*, pp. 76-77.

*And not many furlongs thence
Is your Father's residence.* . . .

With a histrionically exaggerated confession of his presumption in doing so, he would nonetheless prostrate himself at Milton's feet to ask

in a timid whisper whether rhymes and finger-metre do not render poor flat prose ludicrous, rather than tend to elevate it, or even to hide *its nakedness.* [35]

If meter is to be used at all, all else must be, in his frequent phrase for it, *in keeping* with it. And this includes, before all else besides, the language.

As Coleridge conceives it, a prime condition of that "keeping" is a heightened emphasis on the words themselves in the "poematic" as distinct from the prosaic ordonnance. Words are among the chief objects of that attention of which he declares meter to be the stimulant, an attention that assures the reader the fullest realization of their sensuous and semantic qualities. No modern student of poetics will fail to notice the close resemblance of Coleridge's reasoning here to the concept of *foregrounding,* or *deautomatization,* elaborated by the Slavic Formalist critics.

Yet Coleridge's views must be appreciated for what they are in themselves apart from their many anticipations of later speculation. And to this end they must be considered in their own immediate intellectual setting; that is, in relation to the Romantic organic aesthetics of the time, and specifically to the organic version of artistic unity, which Coleridge defines and repeatedly propounds in his critical writings.

Organic unity and Coleridge's theory of verse dic-

[35] *Miscellaneous Criticism*, p. 183.

tion most immediately coincide in his definition of a poem as a species of composition yielding "such delight from the *whole*, as is compatible with a distinct gratification from each component *part*." This organic part-whole relation, as he further explains, is a mean between the complete disunity of a series of striking lines or couplets each of which absorbs the reader's whole attention, and the monolithic unity of "an unsustained composition" whose component parts are devoid of individual attraction. And as usual with Coleridge, the objective structure so described is provided with a subjective, psychological ground:

The reader should be carried forward, not merely or chiefly by the mechanical impulse of curiosity, or by a restless desire to arrive at a final solution; but by the pleasurable activity of mind excited by the attractions of the journey itself.[36]

The full savoring of the details of diction, imagery, syntactic components, and so forth which a sensitive reader enjoys in fine verse is here given a theoretical justification imperfectly realized in the neoclassical notion of unity epitomized in a couplet of Pope's *Essay on Criticism*:

'Tis not a lip or eye we beauty call
But the joint force and full result of all.

To this too partial view of the issue, the organic critic retorts that in fact we *do* call the lip or eye beautiful, just as, simultaneously, we respond to the beauty of the whole which is presupposed by the conjunction of these parts and which each of them contains in germ, as it were.

[36] *Biographia*, II, 10, 11.

Romantic organic aesthetics had its proper home not in England but in Germany, where men like Schiller, the Schlegels, and Schelling were its chief proponents. But it is the description of organic unity given by the philosopher Hegel in his posthumous *Lectures on Aesthetics*, published in the year following Coleridge's death, that deserves notice, if only because the near identity of its terms with those of his English contemporary's definition of a poem has not, I think, been pointed out. The parallel is perhaps the more noteworthy since in this case no influence, in either direction, can be in question.

In a unified work of art, Hegel explains, there must be a particularization of its individual parts, each of which must appear to be cultivated for its own sake in order to attain to organic unity ("um in eine organische Einheit treten zu kommen"). A prose discourse engages the mere understanding ("Verstand") which hurries over details to the *Endresultat* (cf. Coleridge's "final solution") of an intellectual abstraction or a practical purpose. In the mode of thought expressed by poetic discourse, however, and by the part-whole relationship it entails, each part is given independent importance. Every moment is interesting and vibrant for its own sake ("für sich interessant, für sich lebendig") and so the imagination delights to tarry over it, to paint it lovingly, treating it as a totality in itself. Poetry, Hegel's ponderous personifications continue, makes its way more slowly than the judgments and conclusions of the Understanding, which cares contrastingly less for the path along which it travels to its destination ("weniger dagegen auf der Weg, den er entlanggeht"), indifferent, in Coleridge's identical image, to "the attractions of the journey itself."[37]

This piquant analogy between physical and mental

---

[37] *Werke*, 20 vols. (Frankfurt am Main: Suhrkamp Verlag, 1970), XV, *Vorlesungen über die Ästhetik*, 250-251.

progression seems a clear advance over traditional attempts to discriminate the age-old stylistic modes of prose and verse. Not surprisingly, it must be added to the other features of the *Biographia*'s poetics that have been independently confirmed in twentieth-century criticism. The abbé Bremond found the same analogy to be compatible with the poetics of mystical idealism which he elaborated in *La Poésie pure*. To an exquisite passage in a great poem, he wrote, we exclaim, "Stop! let me savor the delights of this beautiful line"; whereas to prose we say impatiently, "Get on with it! Hasten to the outcome" (marche! marche! *Ad eventum festina*). It has a close parallel in the comparison of prose to walking, and poetry to dancing, set forth by Paul Valéry in a lecture delivered at Oxford in 1939. In what he affirmed to be no superficial likeness but a substantial and fruitful analogy, walking and prose, as in Coleridge's image, aim at a final end ("terme fini"). But he differs from Coleridge in conceiving poetry and the dance as entirely nonprogressive, having no "end" beyond their own verbal and bodily movements. This difference between them reflects the greater "purism" of the French poet's theory. If poetic expression pursues any object at all, Valéry declares, it is only an ideal one, and ecstatic state, the phantom of a flower, a smile. The contrasting tendency of current thought to preserve some cognitive and referential status for poetry returns to Coleridge's view that although poetry, too, moves toward a communicative goal, getting there is half—or rather more than half—the fun. "Prose," writes Howard Nemerov in the latest version of the idea, "is a way of getting on, poetry a way of lingering."[38]

[38] Henri Bremond, *La Poésie pure* (Paris, 1926, p. 17). Valéry, *Oeuvres*, 2 vols. (Paris: Gallimard, 1957), I, 1330; Nemerov, "On the Measure of Poetry," *Critical Inquiry*, VI (1979), 338.

Like Coleridge, too, Hegel envisages a poetic structure that avoids the opposite extremes of an undifferentiated unity and a total disunity.

For the autonomy [of each part] must not be so firmly established that it is absolutely disjunct from the others; the independence asserts itself only enough to show the various aspects and portions of the work as having achieved their own vital representative status. . . .

These relatively autonomous parts nonetheless form a whole because the fundamental theme of the work ("Grundbestimmung") is developed and exhibited in each one of them. Whenever poetry deviates from the perfection of this dynamic unity, Hegel declares, its products tend to fall from the region of free fantasy into the realm of prose ("das Bereich der Prosa").[39]

Being themselves mere signs, words lack the immediate representative potential of the sculptor's solid forms or the musician's sensuous tones. Hegel recognizes, however, that as vehicles of poetic representation they must be discriminated from the expressive mode of prose. Conceding that poetic expression would thus appear to be a purely linguistic phenomenon, Hegel nevertheless asserts that the true source of poetic language lies neither in the choice of words nor in their combination into syntactic units, nor even in rhythm, euphony, or rhyme. It consists rather in the species and mode of representation ("der Art und Weise der Vorstellung").

Although Coleridge himself would never have tolerated Hegel's cleavage between the poetic mimetic mode and the prosodic and syntactic features which determine it, his "Weise der Vorstellung" would seem to accord well enough with the English critic's

[39] *Vorlesungen über die Ästhetik*, pp. 252-253. All English quotations from the *Vorlesungen* are my own translations.

idea of an imitation. Moreover, one might plausibly argue that Coleridge's exposition of copy-vs-imitation fairly carries out Hegel's requirement that the analyst must before all else determine the form this *Vorstellung* must take in order to become poetry ("um zu einem poetischen Ausdruck zu kommen").[40]

"This linguistic aspect of poetry," Hegel observes in the *Aesthetic Lectures*, "could provide us with material for endlessly extensive and complex discussions"—a statement which the course of twentieth-century poetics has endowed with something like prophetic force. But he himself preferred to forego the undertaking. Moreover, this and other recognitions of the central place that language must hold in any poetic theory were insufficient to alter his conviction that the essential difference between prose and poetry was conceptual, not stylistic, referable merely to "two different spheres of consciousness" ("zwei unterschiedene Sphären des Bewusstseins"). That phrase is vague enough to have permitted a corresponding linguistic distinction: each kind of mental operation, as many have argued since, may have its expressive mode. But in what hardly seems reconcilable with his own organicism—and in direct contradiction to Coleridge—Hegel goes so far as to declare that a poem suffers no essential loss when translated into another language, or even into prose![41]

Jean Cohen's objection that the German philosopher's *differentia specifica* of poetry, a "modalité de la représentation" (Hegel's "Weise der Vorstellung"), is itself called into being by "un certain langage" is certainly not chargeable against Coleridge. When the mimetic theory that discriminates his imitation from a copy is applied to verse it generates a prosody whose central tenet is a uniquely poetic, or rather *poematic*, linguistic mode. This verbal ordonnance, in

[40] *Ibid.*, p. 275.   [41] *Ibid.*, pp. 283, 244, 229.

turn, is one in which meter, aural devices, and deviant syntax collaborate to raise syntactical and lexical elements from the level of communicative means to aesthetic ends. Thus they answer perfectly to the part-whole relationship of Coleridge's conception of organic unity, in which the pleasure conferred by the whole must consist with a separately felt pleasure from the component parts. In order to reveal itself, he told one of his lecture audiences, the spirit of poetry must take on a living body; "but a living body is of necessity an organized one,—and what is organization, but the connection of parts to a whole, so that each part is at once end and means!" In our own day W. K. Wimsatt similarly taught that "in literature a part is never a means to another part which is the end, or to a whole which is the end—unless in the organistic sense that all parts and the whole are reciprocally ends and means. . . ."[42]

Coleridge's untiring scrutiny of language, including its special poetic function, allowed him to extend the aesthetic organicism of his age in a direction that associates him in yet another respect with the structuralism of Jakobson and Mukařovský. If this affinity needs further demonstration it may be provided by a passage in a lucid analysis of the "Prague School Theory" just published by F. W. Galan.

In poetry. . . . elements that in standard language have only a subservient role acquire a largely autonomous *value, for poetic language is directed toward the verbal sign itself, not the extralinguistic reality. In short, poetry aims at actualization in order to throw into relief the very act of expression.*

The analysis of a literary work, consequently, centers on

---

[42] Cohen, *Structure du langage poétique*, p. 206; *Shakespearean Criticism*, I, 197; Wimsatt, *The Verbal Icon* (Lexington: University of Kentucky Press, 1954), p. 243.

demonstrating the degree of actualization of its component parts.

It is perhaps worth noting as well that the concept of organic or biological unity had some direct influence on the thinking of the Prague School quite early in their deliberations, as Peter Steiner has recently pointed out. Even without it, however, the phenomenological rigor of his linguistic method leads Roman Jakobson to affirm the same autonomy of the component elements of poetic discourse posited by the organicism of Hegel and Coleridge. In poetry, Jakobson writes, "any constituents of the verbal code. . . . carry their own autonomous signification."[43]

[43] Galan, "Literary System and Systematic Change: The Prague School of Literary History, 1928-1948," *PMLA*, XCIV (1979), 277; Steiner, "The Conceptual Basis of Prague Structuralism," in *Sound, Sign and Meaning: Quinquagenary of the Prague Linguistic Circle* (Ann Arbor: The University of Michigan Press, 1978), pp. 352-353; Jakobson, "On Linguistic Aspects of Translation," in *Selected Writings*, 4 vols. (The Hague: Mouton, 1971), II, 266. Mukařovský himself distinguished the structuralist idea of unity from the closed whole of modern "holistic thought." He apparently conceived of it as more specifically Hegelian. The whole envisaged by structuralism, he declared in 1945, is an interplay of forces in a constantly disturbed and restored equilibrium. "Hence the generic kinship of structuralist thought with dialectic logic." "The Concept of the Whole in the Theory of Art," in *Structure, Sign, and Function: Selected Essays of Jan Mukařovský*, trans. and ed. John Burbank and Peter Steiner (New Haven: Yale University Press, 1978), p. 79.

V

Tamers of the Chaos

That Coleridge has been so little recognized as an intellectual ancestor by even the most distinguished proponents of structuralist poetics, European and American alike, at first seems odd. Yet it is possible that some of them, thinking of him chiefly as one of the leading British Romantic poets, left his prose largely unread. Others, perhaps taking their cue from the long indifference of Coleridge's own countrymen to the signal achievement of the *Biographia Literaria*, may have assumed it to be like the bulk of pre-World War I poetics devoid of the analytical precision of their own Saussurean reasoning and therefore negligible.

This neglect, it should be made clear, derogates nothing from what these modern investigators have given us, especially those in the Slavic countries and France, whose discoveries are in no way dependent on Coleridge's example. For this very reason, certain aesthetic principles common to his and their very different analytical procedures, principles on which his definition of poetic language rests, deserve serious attention. In order to refute Wordsworth's superficially plausible dictional naturalism, Coleridge had to ground his own account on a mimetic principle governing all the fine arts. The words of a poem are an imitation of reality, not a copy, worthless unless they differ from the reality they represent.

Admittedly the rather broad terms in which Coleridge formulated his "universal principle" raises a number of subsidiary questions hardly settled in his writings. Exactly what, for example, is the "reality" imitated in a poem—the objects and events alluded to, the poet's thoughts, or (as some modern theorists have it) nonpoetic discourse? At different times he seems to have meant all of these things, without inquiring whether each of them might argue a slightly different conception of the mimetic nexus of word and world. Coleridge's failure to explore this aspect of the problem seems the more strange since writers whom he admired had begun to see that the various media delimit both the objects and the mode of artistic representation. One thinks chiefly of G. E. Lessing's sharp separation of poetry from painting and sculpture in this respect, in *Laokoon*. But even Adam Smith, in the very essay Coleridge drew upon to illustrate his concept of imitation, had at least crudely discriminated among thoughts, passions, formal discourse, and conversation as natural originals imitated with varying degrees of success by poetry, music, and dance.[1]

Nor, for that matter, does Coleridge take sufficient account of the theoretical consequences of his own recognition that prose occupies a middle point of formalization between verse and conversation. He neglects to ask whether prose is not also something other than a mere copy—even if its referential status is generically distinct from the imitational mode of verse. Still, it seems a fair guess that Coleridge would have extended his universal principle at least to imaginative prose if the English novel had by his day been accorded the artistic prestige it was to attain only with the advocacy (and perhaps the example) of Henry

[1] *The Early Writings of Adam Smith*, ed. J. Ralph Lindgren (New York: Augustus M. Kelley, 1967), pp. 153, 156.

James. As it is, we must turn to twentieth-century critics for this extension. Most eminent among several others whose critical imaginations owe something to Coleridge's guidance, T. S. Eliot finds an identity of spoken and written utterance as intolerable in prose as in verse. The older critic could hardly ask for a more faithful description of his *imitation* than the terms in which Eliot characterizes Molly Bloom's long interior monologue at the end of Joyce's *Ulysses*. What Joyce produced, Eliot perceived, is not a model of how men and women actually think, but instead "a very skilful attempt by a master of language to give the illusion of mental process by a different medium, that of written words."[2]

Nonetheless, whatever the restrictions of its application in Coleridge's own criticism, those who would dismiss his crucial separation of copy and imitation, or relegate it to the status of a personal hobby horse trotted irrelevantly into his discussion of poetic language, engage formidable modern opponents. In 1940 Jan Mukařovský published a long essay "On Poetic Language," a brilliant compendium of some years of prior speculation on the problem. Near the end of this piece, considering what he believes to be the poet's aim at a direct presentation of "the course of psychic processes by means of the word," he is led to what amounts to a reformulation of Coleridge's reiterated insistence that poetry is an art and therefore subject to the conditions of a true imitation. "An absolutely exact copy," Mukařovský wrote,

is, of course, out of the question because it is by no means possible to purge language of logical relationships, on the one hand, and because an intrinsic precondition of art is the distance between the material and its artistic recreation, on

---

[2] *Selected Essays* (New York: Harcourt, Brace, 1950), pp. 443-444.

the other. Just as in every solution of an artistic problem, here too we have a mere artistic tendency.[3]

Clearly, the Czech theorist's "intrinsic precondition of art" is another name for Coleridge's "universal principle."

Coleridge's imitation, I've argued above, is an instance of that more fundamental reconciliation of opposites effected by the creative imagination. This reconciliation is anything but peaceful. Because the opposites are polar the reconciliation is dynamic, not static, and thereby productive of a tension felt by the reader of a poem as an essential part of his aesthetic response. In Coleridge's literary aesthetics this notion is ubiquitous, as the opposites reconciled take different forms according to their manifestation in the various stages of the creative process, in the structure of the finished work, and in the psychology of the pleasurable experience it evokes. Meter sets in dynamic opposition the polar extremes of "more than usual" emotion and order, first in the poet and then in his reader. The school of American New Critics early saw in Coleridge's polarity a progenitor of their own notions of poetic paradox, irony, or tension. But the more thoroughgoing formalism of the Slavic investigators more nearly approaches the inclusiveness of Coleridge's concept. In 1933 Mukařovský discovered in verse a "tension of a dual intonational scheme, syntactic and rhythmic," which, constantly felt, distinguishes poetic rhythm from that of prose. But this is only, as so often with Coleridge's thought as well, a single manifestation of an all-pervading characteristic. "The essence of literary structure," Mukařovský observed some years later, "lies in the polar tension

---

[3] *The Word and Verbal Art: Selected Essays by Jan Mukařovský*, trans. and ed. John Burbank and Peter Steiner (New Haven: Yale University Press, 1977), p. 62.

among individual components, the tension that maintains the structure in constant developmental movement." This sentence, the first clause of which reads like a paraphrase of many to be found in Coleridge's criticism, extends polarity to entire literatures, as a prime determinant of their historical evolution.[4]

The idea that a work of art somehow involves an equilibrium of conflicting forces has been among the commonplaces of Western aesthetics since the Romantic age. Art succeeds, as Austin Warren memorably put it, "when there is an equilibrium which is also a tension, when there is a rage waiting to be ordered and a rage to find, or to make, that ordering."[5] Warren's two "rages," we should note, correspond perfectly to Coleridge's two "passions," the one requiring the control of meter and the other supplying it.

The aesthetics of polarity has a special appeal to those critics for whom poetic expression is radically metaphorical. A metaphor forces into unity disparate material, a process often seen to involve a kind of violence, as in Dr. Johnson's familiar description of the metaphysical conceit, in which "the most heterogeneous ideas are yoked by violence together." Although such strained imagery struck Johnson as a perverse stylistic deviation, it has long since won

[4] *Ibid.*, pp. 133, 206.
[5] I have explored the rationale of this concept, including Coleridge's contribution to it, in "The Achieve of, the Mastery . . . , *The Journal of Aesthetics and Art Criticism*, XVI (1957), 103-111. For a well-argued application of it to painting, see Andrew Ushenko's *Dynamics of Art* (Bloomington: Indiana University Press, 1953). Warren, *Rage for Order* (Chicago: University of Chicago Press, 1948), p.v. Richard Schiff has lately identified "the tension of an equilibrium established among a number of forces," so often invoked in describing works of art, as itself a metaphor. See his "Art and Life: A Metaphoric Relationship," *Critical Inquiry*, V (1978), 114-115.

acceptance as the norm of metaphoric structure. "Where there is metaphor," Nelson Goodman writes, "there is conflict. . . ." For Philip Wheelwright the essence of metaphor consists in a "semantic tension" among its heterogeneous elements. Refining on Wheelwright, David S. Miall names the "tensive aspect" as semantically most efficacious among several he discerns in the metaphoric function. Most recently, Paul Ricoeur has identified in the "restructuration of semantic fields" effected by metaphor "a specific kind of tension . . . between semantic incongruence and congruence." All metaphors predicate an equation of unlikes, a process Ricoeur labels *predicative assimilation*. Then he describes its effect:

To see the like is to see the same in spite of, and through, the different. This tension between sameness and difference characterizes the logical structure of likeness. Imagination, accordingly, is this ability to produce new kinds by assimilation and to produce them not above the differences, as in the concept, but in spite of and through the differences. [6]

To the extent that Ricoeur's account of the metaphoric function (now seen to be much more complex than classical rhetoric had represented it to be) is valid, Coleridge's imitation would appear to be essentially metaphorical. The productive imagination involved in the formation of Ricoeur's metaphors is strikingly similar to the faculty that produces Coleridge's imitation, a likeness which "of necessity im-

[6] Goodman, *Languages of Art* (London: Oxford University Press, 1969), p. 69; Wheelwright, *The Burning Fountain: A Study in the Language of Symbolism*, new and rev. ed. (Bloomington: Indiana University Press, 1968), p. 102; David S. Miall, "Metaphor and Literary Meaning," *The British Journal of Aesthetics*, XVII (1977), p. 57; Ricoeur, "The Metaphoric Process as Cognition, Imagination, and Feeling," *Critical Inquiry*, V (1978), 148.

plies and demands difference" and which, in his earliest attempt at defining it (see above, III, 46-47), Coleridge had called a Proteus Essence "known and felt not to be the thing [imitated] by that difference of the Substance which made every atom of the Form another thing—that likeness not identity. . . ." If Ricoeur's imagination is not quite twin brother to Coleridge's famous reconciler of opposites in poetry, it is assuredly a first cousin.

But what most soundly establishes the cogency and lasting appeal of the theory elaborated in the *Biographia* is that it defines metrical utterance in a way that shows it to be central to the poet's art. The techniques of modern linguistic science, applied with unparalleled scrupulosity to verse, have enabled its adherents to provide ingenious dissections of what Jakobson called the "organized violence of poetic form on language."[7] But Coleridge's "salutary antagonism" generated by the metrical control of passion (another avatar of tension) answers to the poets' own intuition of what their creative impulse comes to. Wallace Stevens was not alone among practitioners in perceiving that what the Ancient writers called the *furor poeticus* was a "rage for order." Nor is his arresting phrase merely a romantic refinement of the classical image. In lines addressed to his painter friend Charles Jervas, Pope celebrates the two arts they respectively cultivated:

So just thy skill, so regular my rage.

Of course the author of *Kubla Khan* knew as intimately as anyone else the fine frenzy of verbal song.

[7] Quoted in Stephen Rudy, "Jakobson's Inquiry into Verse and the Emergence of Structural Poetics," in *Sound, Sign and Meaning: Quinquagenary of the Prague Linguistic Circle* (Ann Arbor: University of Michigan Press, 1978), p. 490.

Yet had he not also been an unusually penetrating investigator of language, it is at least doubtful that he would as critic have discovered its operancy in the form and conditions of the poet's very medium. Poetry, he notes, admits even the words which are most peculiar to prose, but the fact that it more often rejects them evinces the *"severer keeping"* exacted by "a more continuous state of Passion."[8] That fact alone, however, yields no more than a partial explanation. Coleridge had the critical acumen to see further that nothing of any worth could result from the spontaneous overflow of emotion itself. He knew there could be no poetry until the violence was "organized," the rage made "regular." Our guess that this knowledge arose irresistibly from his own practice before it was confirmed in later theoretical speculation is reenforced by Herbert Read's excellent essay on Coleridge's drastic revision of *Dejection: An Ode*, accurately titled "The Creative Experience in Poetry." Read shows how the process of recasting the original confessional version of the ode into the formal excellence of the final version was essentially the poet's triumphant struggle to bring his painful and unruly state of personal depression into verbal control.[9]

The pleasure a reader takes in metrical form has its counterpart in this creative experience of the poet. And so an important aspect of Coleridge's poetics is its rejection of the quite mistaken belief that meter is a constraint on the poet, shackling his creativity, an error perpetrated in the eighteenth century, long before the vogue of free verse. On the contrary, the reconciling imagination delights as much in the bridle as in the spur. Poets, runs a notebook entry of 1804,

[8] *Notebooks*, III, entry 3611.

[9] *The Forms of Things Unknown: Essays towards an Aesthetic Philosophy* (New York: Horizon Press, 1960), pp. 124-140.

"are Bridlers by Delight, the Purifiers, they that combine [fancy, imagination, superstition, etc.] with *reason* & order, the true Protoplasts, Gods of Love who tame the chaos."[10]

This sense of what they do with words, as experienced by the poets themselves, apparently transcends the peculiar psychological and epistemological concepts of single cultural eras. Herbert Read's essay closes by quoting some translated lines of a verse *Essay on Literature* by the ancient Chinese master Lu Chi. One of its couplets (surely never seen by the author of *Dejection*) speaks of the poet's rare moments of inspiration:

So acute is the mind in such instants of
    divine comprehension,
What chaos is there that it cannot marshall
    in miraculous order?

A much later statement than the one just cited from the notebooks may be read as a fitting reply to the Chinese poet's rhetorical question. Written on a flyleaf in a copy of Barry Cornwall's *Dramatic Scenes and Other Poems*, published in 1819, it seems also designed to meet the obvious objection that all human perception and *a fortiori* all verbal expression, including the flattest prose, impose order on the chaotic flux of experience. Even if this is so, the world created by the prose of the naturalist or the historian, Coleridge argues, is subsumed and transcended in the higher ordering achieved by the poet's verse. As for the truly great poet, the forger of imitations impossible to confuse with mere copies, the note concludes with what may well be the boldest vindication on

---

[10] The neoclassical revolt against meter is treated in my "In Search of the Godly Language," *Philological Quarterly*, LIV (1975), 289-309. *Notebooks*, II, entry 2355.

record of his verbal superiority: "All other men's worlds (κόσμοι)," Coleridge wrote, "are *his* chaos."[11]

This daring claim returns us to his conception of the poet's social and moral function, touched on earlier in Chapter I. Since this consideration belongs to another large area of Coleridge's poetics, using that term in its most inclusive sense, there is no point in exploring its ramifications here. What is germane to my more restricted topic, however, is how admirably his prosody, even in its technical particularity, consists with the high office and value he assigns to poetry. In the poet's creative struggle to control his private passion by metrical manipulation, as it is described in the *Biographia*, it is not fanciful to see the microcosmic counterpart to his racial burden of mastering the chaos by which civilized human existence feels itself constantly menaced (every poem a *Dunciad*).

In this lofty view of the poet's role, needless to say, Coleridge enjoys no monopoly. Many writers have expressed their faith that what the poet does with words is directly relevant to the most ambitious claims for his ministration to man's spiritual requirements. None bolder, we may suppose, than Shelley's in *A Defence of Poetry*, where he declares poets, whose words burn with "electric life," to be the world's unacknowledged legislators, nourishers of a moral imagination without which human kind would degenerate to a spiritual callousness threatening a relapse into barbarism. In fact Coleridge's arresting metaphor of chaos-taming love gods only expands to cosmic sweep and inclusiveness a conception of the poetic function variously formulated throughout the history of Western letters. In terms that are even more hyperbolic than his, it forms a leitmotif of Shel-

[11] Read, *The Forms of Things Unknown*, p. 135; *Miscellaneous Criticism*, p. 343.

ley's essay. "But mark," Shelley exclaims of what he imagines as the poetic spirit's triumph over the dark ages, "how beautiful an order has sprung from the dust and blood of this fierce chaos!" Although he does not follow Coleridge in positing the relatively lawless nature of nonpoetic verbal orderings of the world, he does assert in very similar vein that in reading poetry we become "inhabitants of a world to which the familiar world is a chaos."

The terms of this chaos-into-order figure are precisely those appropriate to a long-standing analogy between artistic and divine creativity, the poet being conceived, in the Earl of Shaftsbury's graphic eighteenth-century version of it, as a "just Prometheus under Jove." Shelley was quite explicit about it. When the poet creates the universe anew after its periodic "annihilations" by men's blunted sensibilities, we're told, he justifies "that bold and true word of Tasso: *Non merita nome di creatore, se non Iddio ed il Poeta.*"[12]

This deification of the poet had its apogee in the Romantic period of course, Coleridge subscribing to it in common with the more revolutionary of his contemporaries. Viewing it now in historical perspective we can admire how nicely his findings about the language of verse and about the source and use of meter accord with the age's ideal of the chaos-conquering poet. Coleridge's superiority over his fellows in this regard shows most clearly in his frank recognition and theoretical embrace of the antinomy lying at the heart of this ideal. He understood that the chaos of the primordial state, like its microcosmic type in the meter-maker's "more than usual emotion," is necessary to the triumphant order achieved by creative ge-

[12] "Only God and poets deserve to be called creators." *Shelley's Literary and Philosophical Criticism*, ed. John Shawcross (London: Humphrey Milford, 1909), pp. 159, 141, 156.

nius. The chaos is therefore tamed, not destroyed; or, in the more familiar Coleridgean phrase, it is reconciled with its opposite in a dynamic polarity perhaps always more efficacious as process than as product. Coleridge's reasoning includes what would logically follow, that the greatness of the created order is directly proportionate to the depth of the chaos. Great poems, that is poems on great themes, are for this reason always metrically powerful, as according to the theory they *must* be.

The more important point, however, and certainly the one most apposite to the thesis of this study, is not how well Coleridge's prosody harmonizes with the Romantic image of the poet but rather how far it transcends the period of its origin. As the bright vision of the poet's sacred calling has faded in ensuing ages or, more accurately, been replaced by less grandiose conceptions, Coleridge's analysis of the art of verse seems to have lost none of its persuasiveness, seems if anything more compelling than before. This is possible because the earlier view of the poet's place and function has not been entirely abandoned; it has instead undergone a metamorphosis. The direction of the change has been downward, or perhaps inward. If even the most gifted of our twentieth-century poets and their apologists cannot feel themselves up to the Shelleyan assignment of unacknowledged cosmic legislation, they nonetheless experience their craft and offer its wares in terms that merely reduce the assignment to the less ambitious dimensions of the subjective and the individual. Whether or not the chaos is in fact universal, it is *felt* only as personal. "These fragments I have shored against my ruins."

If the doctrine advanced during the 1920s by I. A. Richards (later to pay his own tribute to Coleridge's critical tutelage), that the reading of a poem sets in order the clashing appetencies of the reader's nervous system, seems too clinically reductive, an impoverishment of Coleridge's multifaceted equilibration, there are more satisfactory modern versions. Robert Frost, long acclaimed for his metrical mastery, once described both the making of a poem and its functional value in terms that may stand as a reaffirmation of Coleridge adapted to the altered sensibility of the modern psyche. Frost too felt the passion—he called it "wildness"—involved in poetic composition. And he posed the Coleridgean question. How can this wildness subsist with order, which Frost identifies as "fulfilled theme"? He answers that it is accomplished by "the figure a poem makes," something which

begins in delight and ends in wisdom. . . . It begins in delight, it inclines to the impulse, it assumes direction with the first line laid down, it runs a course of lucky events, and ends in a clarification of life. . . .

The clarification in question is not on the scale of prophetic vision portrayed in Shelley's rhapsodic vindication, not necessarily, Frost cautions, the kind on which sects and cults are founded. It is only "a momentary stay against confusion."[13] Nonetheless, we easily recognize in the modern American poet's testimony the familiar lineaments of Coleridge's "Bridlers by Delight," even though, for complex cultural reasons beyond the scope of this inquiry, their poems may no longer symbolize the victories over a universal chaos to which the Romantics could still aspire.

No matter. The more one tests the techniques by which Coleridge's poetic imitation is brought into being, along with the metrical and linguistic conditions that distinguish it from prose discourse, the

[13] Richards' theory is most fully developed in *Science and Poetry* (1926). Frost, *Selected Prose*, ed. Hyde Cox and Edward Connery Lathem (New York: Holt, Rinehart and Winston, n.d.), p. 18.

more apparent it becomes that they cannot be regarded, like Wordsworth's Preface to *Lyrical Ballads*, as essentially the manifesto of a period style answering to the creative exigencies of the day. The momentary crisis of idiom and sensibility (for it seems to have been both), which we know from the early chapters of the *Biographia* Coleridge keenly experienced as aspiring poet, drove him to push his search beyond the needs of personal artistic accommodation and justification. And so he directed the armed vision of his superb analytical powers on language itself as an artistic medium. He realized, and freely confessed, that a full and final solution of the problem he confronted lay outside the compass of human reason. Yet today, a century and a half after his death, it is more apparent than it has ever been that his efforts resulted in a poetics which further investigation dare not ignore.

Index

Addison, Joseph, 35
Anima Poetae, 45
Apocalypse, 30
Appleyard, J. A., 57-58, 59, 66
Aristotle, 48, 50; *The Poetics*, 44
Arnold, Matthew, 27
Auden, W. H., 63n

Barfield, Owen, 26, 48
Barthes, Roland: *Structural Anthropology*, 21
Baskin, Wade, 21n
Bate, Walter Jackson, xii, 33, 64
Beal, Anthony, 59n
Beer, John, 10
Bible, 84
Boccaccio, Giovanni, 85
Borges, Juan Luis, 75-76
Bremond, Henri: *La Poésie pure*, 91
Brooks, Cleanth, ix
Bruns, Gerald L., 21, 22n, 64
Buffon, Georges-Louis Leclerc de: *Discours sur le style*, 76n
Bühler, Karl: *Sprachetheorie*, 71
Bullock, Michael, 47
Burbank, John, 23n, 95n, 99n
Burke, Edmund: *A Philosophical Enquiry into . . . the Sublime and Beautiful*, 18
Byron, George Gordon, Lord, 28, 63

Caesar, Julius, 19-20
Carreter, Fernando Lázaro, 76
Cary, H. F., 29
Chatman, Seymour, 19n, 65n
Chaucer, Geoffrey: *Troilus and Criseyde*, 72

Index

Coburn, Kathleen, 6n, 7n, 12, 45, 80n
Cohen, Jean, 24n, 74 and note, 77, 83, 87, 93
Coleridge, Edward, 34, 78
Coleridge, Ernest Hartley, 45n
Coleridge, Hartley, 29n
Coleridge, Samuel Taylor: *Biographia Literaria*, x, xi, 5, 8, 12n, 17, 19, 22, 26, 34-42 *passim*, 48, 57, 66, 69, 71, 72, 77, 79-80, 91, 96, 102, 105, 109; "Dejection: An Ode," 103, 104; *The Friend*, 6, 8; "Kubla Khan," 102; *Lay Sermons*, 32; *Logic* (manuscript), 9; *Osorio*, 32; "On Poesy or Art," 49-50, 55; "Principles of Genial Criticism," 8; "The Rime of the Ancient Mariner," 38; *The Statesman's Manual*, 16, 19n, 30-31, 64; *Table Talk*, 23n, 60
Coleridge, Sara, 12n
Collingwood, R. G., 64
Collins, William, 38, 39n
Cornwall, Barry, 104
Cox, Hyde, 108n
Culler, Jonathan, 81n

Daniel, Samuel: *Civil Wars*, 73; "Hymen's Triumph," 73
Dante Alighieri, 17, 41; *Divine Comedy* (H. F. Cary translation), 29
Davy, Humphry, 13
De Quincey, Thomas, 6, 83
Descartes, René, 9
Dickens, Charles, 73
Dryden, John, 29, 32n, 46-47, 74
Dufrenne, Mikel, 25, 74n, 83

Eliot, T. S., x, xi, 15-16, 17 and note, 23, 27, 30, 32n, 37, 41, 68, 72, 75, 82, 98; "Burnt Norton," 31; *Four Quartets*, 31; "Little Gidding," 31; "The Music of Poetry," 23; "The Social Function of Poetry," 15; *The Waste Land* (quoted), 107
Emerson, Ralph Waldo, 85
Engell, James, xii
Epictetus, 8, 19

Frost, Robert, 108

Index

Frye, Northrop, 44, 75

Galan, F. W., 94
Gardner, Helen, 31, 32n
Genette, Gérard, 27
Gillman, James, Dr., 12
Gillman, James, Jr., 14, 20
Giovanni, Norman di, 76n
Godwin, William, 8, 9, 17, 22
Goodman, Nelson, 101
Graves, Robert, 83
Gray, Thomas: "Ode on . . . Eton College," 35
Greville, Fulke, 85
Griggs, Earl Leslie, 5n
Gross, Harvey, 83n
Guillen, Jorge, 74

Halpern, Daniel, 76n
Hazlitt, William, 13
Hegel, Georg Wilhelm Friedrich, 95; *Lectures on Aesthetics*, 90, 92-93
Herbert, George, 38, 72-73; "The Flower," 38; "Virtue," 39n
Hill, Archibald A., 25, 74n
Hobbes, Thomas, 8
Hollander, John, 75
Howard, Robert, 46
Hudson, Miss, 63
Hurwitz, Hyman, 9

Ibsen, Henrik, 62
Isaiah, 77

Jakobson, Roman, 6, 10, 19-20, 27, 70-71, 73, 83, 94, 95
James, Henry, 51, 97-98
Jervas, Charles, 102
Jespersen, Otto, 13 and note
Johnson, Samuel, 48, 82, 100
Jonson, Ben: *Bartholomew Fair*, 46
Joyce, James: *Ulysses*, 98

Index

Jung, Carl, 58-59

Kant, Immanuel, 61, 64
Keats, John, 41
Ker, W. P., 47n
Krieger, Murray, 56-57

Landor, Walter Savage, 83
Lathem, Edward Connery, 108n
Lawrence, D. H., 59
Leavis, F. R., 67
Lessing, Gotthold Ephraim: *Laokoon*, 97
Levin, Samuel R., 19n, 65n, 83
Lindgren, Ralph, 53n, 97n
Lévi-Strauss, Claude: *Structural Anthropology*, 21
Locke, John, 9
Logosophia, 9, 10
Lu Chi: *Essay on Literature*, 104
Lukács, Georg, 62

MacKenna, Stephen, 50n
MacKinnon, Donald, 31-32
MacShane, Frank, 76n
Marino, G. B., 34
Mathews, Charles, 62-63
Mendelssohn, Moses, 52-56
Miall, David S., 101
Milton, John, 12, 29, 30, 85; *Comus*, 79, 87-88; *Paradise Lost*, 79, 82
Molière (Jean-Baptiste Poquelin), 75
Molina, Juan Ignacio, 13
Mudford, William, 18
Mukařovský, Jan, 23, 25, 94, 98-100
Murray, John, 7

Nemerov, Howard, 91
North, Thomas: *Plutarch's Lives* (trans.), 79

Olson, Charles, 75
Orsini, G.N.G., 50, 56-57

Index

Osgood, Charles G., 85n
Ovid, 68

Page, B. S., 50n
Pater, Walter, 24, 27
Plato, 10, 16, 48; *The Republic*, 44
Plotinus, 54; *The Enneads*, 50
Poe, Edgar A., 24, 85
Poole, Thomas, 15
Pope, Alexander, 28, 41, 84, 85, 86-87, 102; *The Dunciad*, 105; "An Epistle to Dr. Arbuthnot," 68; *An Essay on Criticism*, 89; *An Essay on Man*, 31; *Moral Essays*, 86
Pound, Ezra, 38
Prescott, Frederick Clarke, 67n

Ransom, John Crowe, 44, 67, 68, 81n
Raysor, Thomas M., 12n, 48, 61n
Read, Herbert, 10n, 83, 103, 104
Reynolds, Joshua: *Discourses on Art*, 51-52
Richards, I. A., 27, 50n, 83, 107, 108n
Ricoeur, Paul, 101-102
Robinson, Henry Crabb, 29
Robinson, Mary: "The Haunted Beach," 29
Rooke, Barbara, 6n, 9
Rousseau, Jean-Jacques, 42
Rudy, Stephen, 102n
Ruskin, John, 83

Saint John, Gospel of, 10
Sapir, Edward, 7, 82
Saussure, Ferdinand de, 6, 10, 22; *Cours de linguistique générale*, 20-21
Schelling, Friedrich, 45-50, 54, 90; "Concerning the Relation of the Plastic Arts to Nature," 47-48, 49, 61n; *Philosophische Schriften*, 45; *Transcendental Idealism*, 49
Scherer, Edmond, xi
Schiff, Richard, 100n
Schiller, Friedrich, 80n, 90
Schlegel, August Wilhelm, 36, 90
Schlegel, Friedrich, 90

Index

Scholes, Robert, 20, 21n, 26
Scott, Walter: *The Lady of the Lake*, 81
Sebeok, Thomas A., 84n
Sennert, Daniel, 8
Shaftesbury, Anthony Cooper, third Earl of, 106
Shakespeare, William, 12-13, 23-24, 29, 35-36, 51, 58, 61, 63, 64-65, 66, 79, 81-82; *Hamlet*, 23, 24, 35, 36, 58; *Love's Labour's Lost*, 24; *Macbeth*, 29; *Richard II*, 12; *Romeo and Juliet*, 36; *The Tempest*, 12, 65
Shawcross, John, 8n, 45, 50n, 106n
Shelley, Percy Bysshe, 41, 107, 108; *A Defence of Poetry*, 105-106; *Prometheus Unbound*, 7
Smith, Adam, 52-53, 55-56, 97
Smith, Barbara H., 44
Snyder, Alice D., 9-10, 10n, 16
Sotheby, William, 5, 30, 70
Southey, Robert, 11, 30, 32, 38, 79
Spenser, Edmund: "Epithalamium," 29; "Hymn of Heavenly Beauty," 85
Stankiewicz, Edward, 84
Steiner, George, 10
Steiner, Peter, 23n, 95 and note, 99n
Stevens, Wallace, 102
Strozzi, Giovambattista, 19
Stuart, Daniel, 8

Tasso, Torquato, 106
Tate, Allen, 77, 78
Tennyson, Alfred, Lord, 28
Thomson, James, 30
Todorov, Tzetvan, 6, 26-27
Tomalin, J., 84

Ushenko, Andrew, 100n

Valéry, Paul, 7, 83, 91
Van Gogh, Vincent, 59
Van Huysum, Jacob, 53, 62
Vico, Giambattista, 10
Virgil, 28

Index

Wark, Robert R., 52n
Warren, Austin, 100
Warton, Joseph, 86
Warton, Thomas, 79
Wedgwood, Josiah, 9
Wedgwood, Thomas, 13n, 32
Wellek, René, 20n, 53n
Wheelwright, Philip, 65, 101
White, R. J., 16n, 32
Wieland, Christoph Martin; *Oberon*, 30
Wimsatt, William K., ix, 25, 94
Winckelmann, Johann Joachim, 50-51, 54
Wordsworth, William, 5, 25, 26, 28-29, 30, 35, 42-43, 57, 72, 76-77, 81, 87, 96; "Alice Fell," 81; *Lyrical Ballads*, 17n, 33; Preface to *Lyrical Ballads*, 6, 28, 32, 73, 86, 109; "The Sailor's Mother," 81; "Simon Lee," 81
Wright, Patience, 53

Yeats, W. B., 32; "Adam's Curse," 41
Young, Edward, 87n

Princeton Essays in Literature

The Orbit of Thomas Mann. By Erich Kahler

On Four Modern Humanists: Hofmannsthal, Gundolf, Curtius, Kantorowicz. Edited by Arthur R. Evans, Jr.

Flaubert and Joyce: The Rite of Fiction. By Richard Cross

A Stage for Poets: Studies in the Theatre of Hugo and Musset. By Charles Affron

Hofmannsthal's Novel "Andreas." By David H. Miles

Kazantzakis and the Linguistic Revolution in Greek Literature. By Peter Bien

Modern Greek Writers. Edited by Edmund Keeley and Peter Bien

On Gide's Prométhée: Private Myth and Public Mystification. By Kurt Weinberg

The Inner Theatre of Recent French Poetry. By Mary Ann Caws

Wallace Stevens and the Symbolist Imagination. By Michel Benamou

Cervantes' Christian Romance: A Study of "Persiles y Sigismunda." By Alban K. Forcione

The Prison-House of Language: a Critical Account of Structuralism and Formalism. By Frederic Jameson

Ezra Pound and the Troubadour Tradition. By Stuart Y. McDougal

Wallace Stevens: Imagination and Faith. By Adalaide K. Morris

On the Art of Medieval Arabic Literature. By Andras Hamori

The Poetic World of Boris Pasternak. By Olga Hughes

The Aesthetics of György Lukács. By Béla Királyfalvi

The Echoing Wood of Theodore Roethke. By Jenijoy La Belle

Achilles' Choice: Examples of Modern Tragedy. By David Lenson

The Figure of Faust in Valéry and Goethe. By Kurt Weinberg

The Situation of Poetry: Contemporary Poetry and Its Traditions. By Robert Pinsky

The Symbolic Imagination: Coleridge and the Romantic Tradition. By J. Robert Barth, S.J.

Adventures in the Deeps of the Mind: The Cuchulain Cycle of W. B. Yeats. By Barton R. Friedman

Shakespearean Representation: Mimesis and Modernity in Elizabethan Tragedy. By Howard Felperin

René Char: The Myth and the Poem. By James R. Lawler

The German Bildungsroman from Wieland to Hesse. By Martin Swales

Six French Poets of Our Time: A Critical and Historical Study. By Robert W. Greene

Coleridge's Metaphors of Being. By Edward Kessler

The Lost Center and Other Essays in Greek Poetry. By Zissimos Lorenzatos

Shakespeare's Revisions of KING LEAR. By Steven Urkowitz

Language and Logos in Boswell's Life of Johnson. By William C. Dowling

Coleridge on the Language of Verse. By Emerson R. Marks

Library of Congress Cataloging in Publication Data

Marks, Emerson R
 Coleridge on the language of verse.

 (Princeton essays in literature)
 Includes bibliographical references and index.
 1. Coleridge, Samuel Taylor, 1772-1834—
Aesthetics. 2. Poetics. I. Title.
PR4487.A35M37   801'.951   80-8562
ISBN 0-691-06458-4

Emerson Marks is Professor of English at the University of Massachusetts, Boston, and the author of *Relativist and Absolutist: The Early Neoclassical Debate in England* and *The Poetics of Reason: Neoclassical Criticism* (Random House). He has also translated the literary criticism of Sainte-Beuve.